Selectors, Specificity, and the Cascade

Eric A. Meyer

O'REILLY®

Beijing · Cambridge · Farnham · Köln · Sebastopol · Tokyo

Selectors, Specificity, and the Cascade

by Eric A. Meyer

Published by O'Reilly Media, Inc., 1005 Gravenstein Highway North, Sebastopol, CA 95472.

O'Reilly books may be purchased for educational, business, or sales promotional use. Online editions are also available for most titles (*http://my.safaribooksonline.com*). For more information, contact our corporate/institutional sales department: 800-998-9938 or *corporate@oreilly.com*.

Editors: Simon St. Laurent and Meghan Blanchette **Cover Designer:** Karen Montgomery
Production Editor: Kristen Borg **Interior Designer:** David Futato
Copyeditor: Rachel Leach **Illustrator:** Robert Romano
Proofreader: O'Reilly Production Services

Revision History for the First Edition:
   2012-09-25   First release
See *http://oreilly.com/catalog/errata.csp?isbn=9781449342494* for release details.

ISBN: 978-1-449-34249-4

[LSI]

1348245323

Table of Contents

Preface

Conventions Used in This Book

The following typographical conventions are used in this book:

Italic

> Indicates new terms, URLs, email addresses, filenames, and file extensions.

`Constant width`

> Used for program listings, as well as within paragraphs to refer to program elements such as variable or function names, databases, data types, environment variables, statements, and keywords.

`Constant width bold`

> Shows commands or other text that should be typed literally by the user.

`Constant width italic`

> Shows text that should be replaced with user-supplied values or by values determined by context.

 This icon signifies a tip, suggestion, or general note.

 This icon indicates a warning or caution.

Using Code Examples

This book is here to help you get your job done. In general, you may use the code in this book in your programs and documentation. You do not need to contact us for permission unless you're reproducing a significant portion of the code. For example, writing a program that uses several chunks of code from this book does not require permission. Selling or distributing a CD-ROM of examples from O'Reilly books does require permission. Answering a question by citing this book and quoting example code does not require permission. Incorporating a significant amount of example code from this book into your product's documentation does require permission.

We appreciate, but do not require, attribution. An attribution usually includes the title, author, publisher, and ISBN. For example: *Selectors, Specificity, and the Cascade* by Eric A. Meyer (O'Reilly). Copyright 2012 O'Reilly Media, Inc., 978-1-449-34249-4."

If you feel your use of code examples falls outside fair use or the permission given above, feel free to contact us at *permissions@oreilly.com*.

Safari® Books Online

Safari Books Online (*www.safaribooksonline.com*) is an on-demand digital library that delivers expert content in both book and video form from the world's leading authors in technology and business.

Technology professionals, software developers, web designers, and business and creative professionals use Safari Books Online as their primary resource for research, problem solving, learning, and certification training.

Safari Books Online offers a range of product mixes and pricing programs for organizations, government agencies, and individuals. Subscribers have access to thousands of books, training videos, and prepublication manuscripts in one fully searchable database from publishers like O'Reilly Media, Prentice Hall Professional, Addison-Wesley Professional, Microsoft Press, Sams, Que, Peachpit Press, Focal Press, Cisco Press, John Wiley & Sons, Syngress, Morgan Kaufmann, IBM Redbooks, Packt, Adobe Press, FT Press, Apress, Manning, New Riders, McGraw-Hill, Jones & Bartlett, Course Technology, and dozens more. For more information about Safari Books Online, please visit us online.

How to Contact Us

Please address comments and questions concerning this book to the publisher:

O'Reilly Media, Inc.
1005 Gravenstein Highway North
Sebastopol, CA 95472
800-998-9938 (in the United States or Canada)
707-829-0515 (international or local)
707-829-0104 (fax)

We have a web page for this book, where we list errata, examples, and any additional information. You can access this page at *http://oreil.ly/selector-specificity-cascade*.

To comment or ask technical questions about this book, send email to *bookquestions@oreilly.com*.

For more information about our books, courses, conferences, and news, see our website at *http://www.oreilly.com*.

Find us on Facebook: *http://facebook.com/oreilly*

Follow us on Twitter: *http://twitter.com/oreillymedia*

Watch us on YouTube: *http://www.youtube.com/oreillymedia*

CHAPTER 1

Selectors

One of the primary advantages of CSS—particularly to designers—is its ability to easily apply a set of styles to all elements of the same type. Unimpressed? Consider this: by editing a single line of CSS, you can change the colors of all your headings. Don't like the blue you're using? Change that one line of code, and they can all be purple, yellow, maroon, or any other color you desire. That lets you, the designer, focus on design, rather than grunt work. The next time you're in a meeting and someone wants to see headings with a different shade of green, just edit your style and hit Reload. *Voilà!* The results are accomplished in seconds and there for everyone to see.

Of course, CSS can't solve all your problems—you can't use it to change the colorspace of your PNGs, for example, at least not yet—but it can make some global changes much easier. So let's begin with selectors and structure.

Basic Style Rules

As stated, a central feature of CSS is its ability to apply certain rules to an entire set of element types in a document. For example, let's say that you want to make the text of all h2 elements appear gray. Using old-school HTML, you'd have to do this by inserting `<FONT COLOR="gray">...</FONT>` tags in all your h2 elements:

```
<h2><font color="gray">This is h2 text</font></h2>
```

Obviously, this is a tedious process if your document contains a lot of h2 elements. Worse, if you later decide that you want all those h2s to be green instead of gray, you'd have to start the manual tagging all over again. (Yes, this is really how it used to be done!)

CSS allows you to create rules that are simple to change, edit, and apply to all the text elements you define (the next section will explain how these rules work). For example, simply write this rule once to make all your h2 elements gray:

```
h2 {color: gray;}
```

If you want to change all h2 text to another color—say, silver—simply alter the value:

```
h2 {color: silver;}
```

Element Selectors

An element selector is most often an HTML element, but not always. For example, if a CSS file contains styles for an XML document, element selectors might look something like this:

```
QUOTE {color: gray;}
BIB {color: red;}
BOOKTITLE {color: purple;}
MYElement {color: red;}
```

In other words, the elements of the document serve as the most basic selectors. In XML, a selector could be anything, since XML allows for the creation of new markup languages that can have just about anything as an element name. If you're styling an HTML document, on the other hand, the selector will generally be one of the many HTML elements such as p, h3, em, a, or even html itself. For example:

```
html {color: black;}
h1 {color: gray;}
h2 {color: silver;}
```

The results of this style sheet are shown in Figure 1-1.

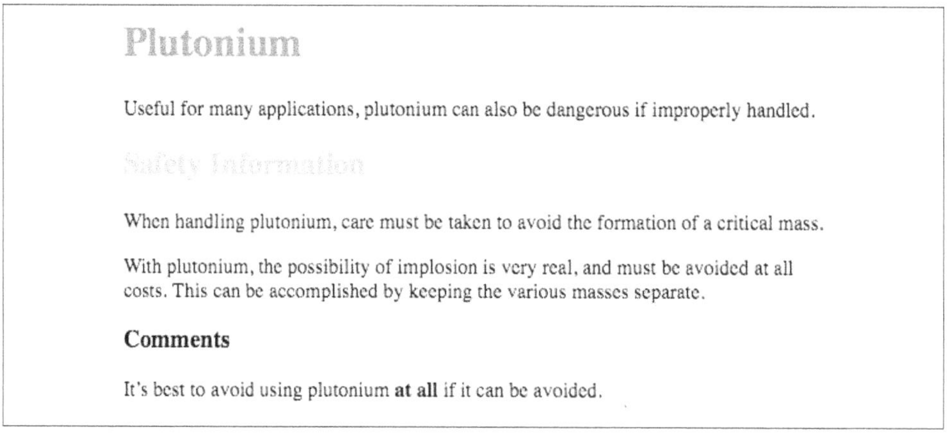

Figure 1-1. Simple styling of a simple document

Once you've globally applied styles directly to elements, you can shift those styles from one element to another. Let's say you decide that the paragraph text, not the h1 elements, in Figure 1-1 should be gray. No problem. Simply change the h1 selector to p:

```
html {color: black;}
p {color: gray;}
h2 {color: silver;}
```

The results are shown in Figure 1-2.

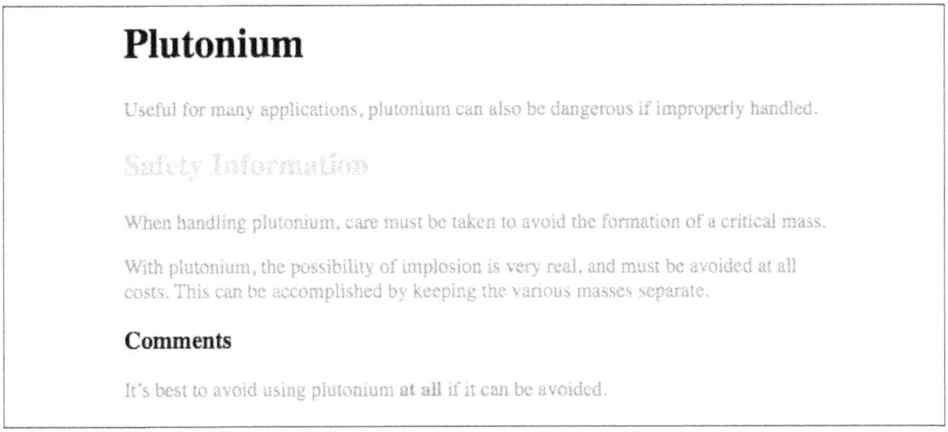

Plutonium

Useful for many applications, plutonium can also be dangerous if improperly handled.

Safety Information

When handling plutonium, care must be taken to avoid the formation of a critical mass.

With plutonium, the possibility of implosion is very real, and must be avoided at all costs. This can be accomplished by keeping the various masses separate.

Comments

It's best to avoid using plutonium at all if it can be avoided.

Figure 1-2. Moving a style from one element to another

Declarations and Keywords

The declaration block contains one or more declarations. A declaration is always formatted as a *property* followed by a colon and then a *value* followed by a semicolon. The colon and semicolon can be followed by zero or more spaces. In nearly all cases, a value is either a single keyword or a space-separated list of one or more keywords that are permitted for that property. If you use an incorrect property or value in a declaration, the whole rule will be ignored. Thus, the following two declarations would fail:

```
brain-size: 2cm;   /* unknown property 'brain-size' */
color: ultraviolet;  /* unknown value 'ultraviolet' */
```

In an instance where you can use more than one keyword for a property's value, the keywords are usually separated by spaces. Not every property can accept multiple keywords, but many, such as the font property, can. Let's say you want to define medium-sized Helvetica for paragraph text, as illustrated in Figure 1-3.

The rule would read as follows:

```
p {font: medium Helvetica;}
```

Note the space between medium and Helvetica, each of which is a keyword (the first is the font's size and the second is the actual font name). The space allows the user agent to distinguish between the two keywords and apply them correctly. The semicolon indicates that the declaration has been concluded.

These space-separated words are referred to as keywords because, taken together, they form the value of the property in question. For instance, consider the following fictional rule:

```
rainbow: red orange yellow green blue indigo violet;
```

There is no such property as rainbow, of course, but the example is useful for illustrative purposes. The value of rainbow is red orange yellow green blue indigo violet, and

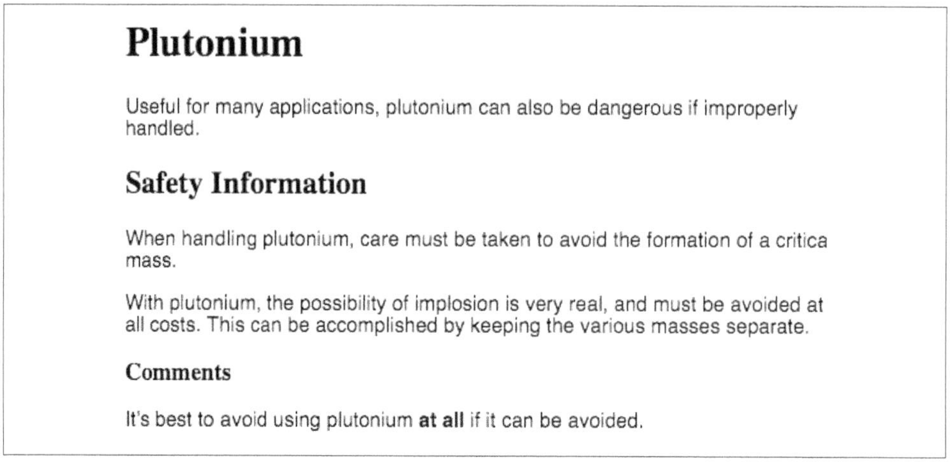

Plutonium

Useful for many applications, plutonium can also be dangerous if improperly handled.

Safety Information

When handling plutonium, care must be taken to avoid the formation of a critica mass.

With plutonium, the possibility of implosion is very real, and must be avoided at all costs. This can be accomplished by keeping the various masses separate.

Comments

It's best to avoid using plutonium **at all** if it can be avoided.

Figure 1-3. The results of a property value with multiple keywords

the seven keywords add up to a single, unique value. We can redefine the value for `rainbow` as follows:

```
rainbow: infrared red orange yellow green blue indigo violet ultraviolet;
```

Now we have a new value for `rainbow` composed of nine keywords instead of seven. Although the two values look mostly the same, they are as unique and different as zero and one. This may seem an abstract point, but it's critical to understanding some of the subtler effects of specificity and the cascade (covered in later in this book).

 There are a few exceptions to the space-separation rule, most of them having come aboard in CSS3. Originally, there was but one exception: the forward slash (/) permitted in the value of `font`. Now there are several instances of symbols like that being used in values, as well as comma-separated lists of values for certain properties.

Those are the basics of simple declarations, but they can get much more complex. The next section begins to show you just how powerful CSS can be.

Grouping

So far, we've seen fairly simple techniques for applying a single style to a single selector. But what if you want the same style to apply to multiple elements? If that's the case, you'll want to use more than one selector or apply more than one style to an element or group of elements.

Grouping Selectors

Let's say you want both h2 elements and paragraphs to have gray text. The easiest way to accomplish this is to use the following declaration:

```
h2, p {color: gray;}
```

By placing the h2 and p selectors on the left side of the rule and separating them with a comma, you've defined a rule where the style on the right (color: gray;) applies to the elements referenced by both selectors. The comma tells the browser that there are two different selectors involved in the rule. Leaving out the comma would give the rule a completely different meaning, which we'll explore later in "Descendant Selectors" on page 24.

There are really no limits to how many selectors you can group together. For example, if you want to display a large number of elements in gray, you might use something like the following rule:

```
body, table, th, td, h1, h2, h3, h4, p, pre, strong, em, b, i {color: gray;}
```

Grouping allows an author to drastically compact certain types of style assignments, which makes for a shorter style sheet. The following alternatives produce exactly the same result, but it's pretty obvious which one is easier to type:

```
h1 {color: purple;}
h2 {color: purple;}
h3 {color: purple;}
h4 {color: purple;}
h5 {color: purple;}
h6 {color: purple;}

h1, h2, h3, h4, h5, h6 {color: purple;}
```

Grouping allows for some interesting choices. For example, all of the groups of rules in the following example are equivalent—each merely shows a different way of grouping both selectors and declarations:

```
/* group 1 */
h1 {color: silver; background: white;}
h2 {color: silver; background: gray;}
h3 {color: white; background: gray;}
h4 {color: silver; background: white;}
b {color: gray; background: white;}

/* group 2 */
h1, h2, h4 {color: silver;}
h2, h3 {background: gray;}
h1, h4, b {background: white;}
h3 {color: white;}
b {color: gray;}

/* group 3 */
h1, h4 {color: silver; background: white;}
h2 {color: silver;}
```

```
h3 {color: white;}
h2, h3 {background: gray;}
b {color: gray; background: white;}
```

Any of these will yield the result shown in Figure 1-4. (These styles use grouped declarations, which are explained in an upcoming section, "Grouping Declarations" on page 6.)

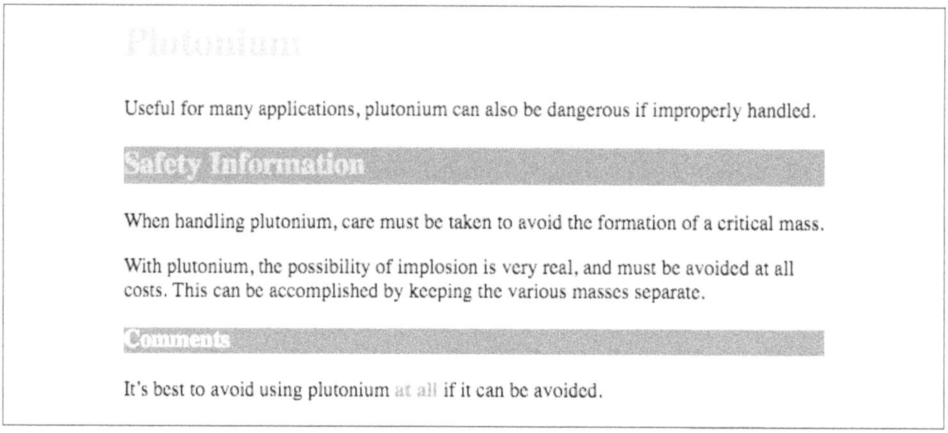

Figure 1-4. The result of equivalent style sheets

The universal selector

CSS2 introduced a new simple selector called the *universal selector*, displayed as an asterisk (*). This selector matches any element at all, much like a wildcard. For example, to make every single element in a document red, you would write:

```
* {color: red;}
```

This declaration is equivalent to a grouped selector that lists every single element contained within the document. The universal selector lets you assign the `color` value `red` to every element in the document in one efficient stroke. Beware, however: although the universal selector is convenient, it can have unintended consequences, which are discussed later in this book.

Grouping Declarations

Since you can group selectors together into a single rule, it follows that you can also group declarations. Assuming that you want all `h1` elements to appear in purple, 18-pixel-high Helvetica text on an aqua background (and you don't mind blinding your readers), you could write your styles like this:

```
h1 {font: 18px Helvetica;}
h1 {color: purple;}
h1 {background: aqua;}
```

But this method is inefficient—imagine creating such a list for an element that will carry 10 or 15 styles! Instead, you can group your declarations together:

```
h1 {font: 18px Helvetica; color: purple; background: aqua;}
```

This will have exactly the same effect as the three-line style sheet just shown.

Note that using semicolons at the end of each declaration is crucial when you're grouping them. Browsers ignore whitespace in style sheets, so the user agent must rely on correct syntax to parse the style sheet. You can fearlessly format styles like the following:

```
h1 {
    font: 18px Helvetica;
    color: purple;
    background: aqua;
}
```

If the second semicolon is omitted, however, the user agent will interpret the style sheet as follows:

```
h1 {
    font: 18px Helvetica;
    color: purple background: aqua;
}
```

Because `background:` is not a valid value for `color`, and because `color` can be given only one keyword, a user agent will ignore the `color` declaration (including the `background: aqua` part) entirely. You might think the browser would at least render h1s as purple text without an aqua background, but if the browser is programmed at all correctly, you won't even get purple h1s. Instead, they will be the default color (which is usually black) with a transparent background (which is also a default). The declaration `font: 18px Helvetica` will still take effect since it was correctly terminated with a semicolon.

 Although it is not technically necessary to follow the last declaration of a rule with a semicolon, it is generally good practice to do so. First, it will keep you in the habit of terminating your declarations with semicolons, the lack of which is one of the most common causes of rendering errors. Second, if you decide to add another declaration to a rule, you won't have to worry about forgetting to insert an extra semicolon. Avoid both problems—always follow a declaration with a semicolon, wherever the rule appears.

As with selector grouping, declaration grouping is a convenient way to keep your style sheets short, expressive, and easy to maintain.

Grouping Everything

You now know that you can group selectors and you can group declarations. By combining both kinds of grouping in single rules, you can define very complex styles using only a few statements. Now, what if you want to assign some complex styles to all the headings in a document, and you want the same styles to be applied to all of them? Here's how to do it:

```
h1, h2, h3, h4, h5, h6 {color: gray; background: white; padding: 0.5em;
    border: 1px solid black; font-family: Charcoal, sans-serif;}
```

You've grouped the selectors, so the styles on the right side of the rule will be applied to all the headings listed; grouping the declarations means that all of the listed styles will be applied to the selectors on the left side of the rule. The result of this rule is shown in Figure 1-5.

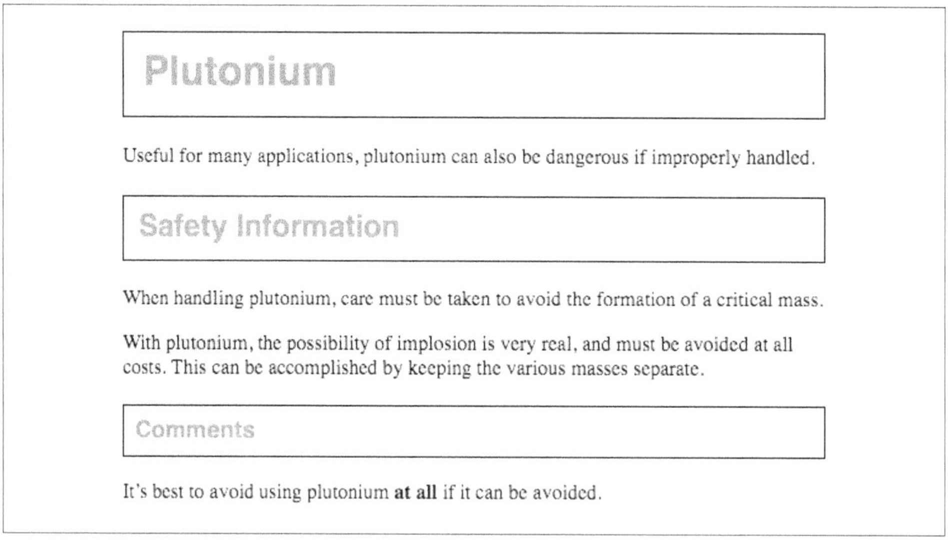

Figure 1-5. Grouping both selectors and rules

This approach is preferable to the drawn-out alternative, which would begin with something like this:

```
h1 {color: gray;}
h2 {color: gray;}
h3 {color: gray;}
h4 {color: gray;}
h5 {color: gray;}
h6 {color: gray;}
h1 {background: white;}
h2 {background: white;}
h3 {background: white;}
```

...and continue for many lines. You *can* write out your styles the long way, but I wouldn't recommend it—editing them would be as tedious as using font tags everywhere!

It's possible to add even more expression to selectors and to apply styles in a way that cuts across elements in favor of types of information. Of course, to get something so powerful, you'll have to do a little work in return, but it's well worth it.

Class and ID Selectors

So far, we've been grouping selectors and declarations together in a variety of ways, but the selectors we've been using are very simple ones that refer only to document elements. They're fine up to a point, but there are times when you need something a little more specialized.

In addition to raw document elements, there are *class selectors* and *ID selectors*, which let you assign styles in a way that is independent of document elements. These selectors can be used on their own or in conjunction with element selectors. However, they work only if you've marked up your document appropriately, so using them generally involves a little forethought and planning.

For example, say you're drafting a document that discusses ways of handling plutonium. The document contains various warnings about safely dealing with such a dangerous substance. You want each warning to appear in boldface text so that it will stand out. However, you don't know which elements these warnings will be. Some warnings could be entire paragraphs, while others could be a single item within a lengthy list or a small section of text. So, you can't define a rule using element selectors of any kind. Suppose you tried this route:

```
p {font-weight: bold;}
```

All paragraphs would be bold, not just those that contain warnings. You need a way to select only the text that contains warnings, or more precisely, a way to select only those elements that are warnings. How do you do it? You apply styles to parts of the document that have been marked in a certain way, independent of the elements involved, by using class selectors.

Class Selectors

The most common way to apply styles without worrying about the elements involved is to use class selectors. Before you can use them, however, you need to modify your actual document markup so that the class selectors will work. Enter the `class` attribute:

```
<p class="warning">When handling plutonium, care must be taken to avoid
the formation of a critical mass.</p>
<p>With plutonium, <span class="warning">the possibility of implosion is
very real, and must be avoided at all costs</span>. This can be accomplished
by keeping the various masses separate.</p>
```

To associate the styles of a class selector with an element, you must assign a `class` attribute to the appropriate value. In the previous code, a class value of `warning` was assigned to two elements: the first paragraph and the span element in the second paragraph.

All you need now is a way to apply styles to these classed elements. In HTML documents, you can use a very compact notation where the name of a class is preceded by a period (.) and can be joined with an element selector:

```
*.warning {font-weight: bold;}
```

When combined with the example markup shown earlier, this simple rule has the effect shown in Figure 1-6. That is, the declaration font-weight: bold will be applied to every element (thanks to the presence of the universal selector) that carries a class attribute with a value of warning.

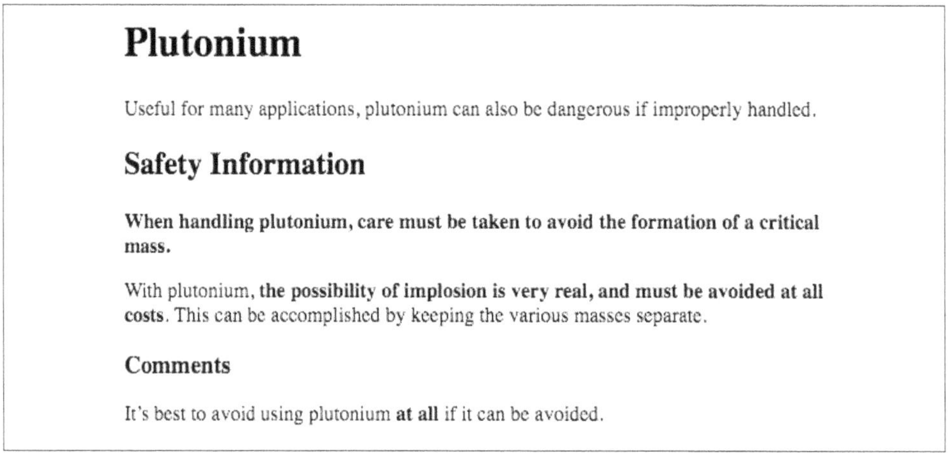

Plutonium

Useful for many applications, plutonium can also be dangerous if improperly handled.

Safety Information

When handling plutonium, care must be taken to avoid the formation of a critical mass.

With plutonium, **the possibility of implosion is very real, and must be avoided at all costs**. This can be accomplished by keeping the various masses separate.

Comments

It's best to avoid using plutonium **at all** if it can be avoided.

Figure 1-6. Using a class selector

As you can see, the class selector works by directly referencing a value that will be found in the class attribute of an element. This reference is *always* preceded by a period (.), which marks it as a class selector. The period helps keep the class selector separate from anything with which it might be combined—such as an element selector. For example, you may want boldface text only when an entire paragraph is a warning:

```
p.warning {font-weight: bold;}
```

The selector now matches any p elements that have a class attribute containing the word warning, but no other elements of any kind, classed or otherwise. Since the span element is not a paragraph, the rule's selector doesn't match it, and it won't be displayed using boldfaced text.

If you did want to assign different styles to the span element, you could use the selector span.warning:

```
p.warning {font-weight: bold;}
span.warning {font-style: italic;}
```

In this case, the warning paragraph is boldfaced, while the warning span is italicized. Each rule applies only to a specific type of element/class combination, so it does not leak over to other elements.

Another option is to use a combination of a general class selector and an element-specific class selector to make the styles even more useful, as in the following markup:

```
.warning {font-style: italic;}
span.warning {font-weight: bold;}
```

The results are shown in Figure 1-7.

Plutonium

Useful for many applications, plutonium can also be dangerous if improperly handled.

Safety Information

When handling plutonium, care must be taken to avoid the formation of a critical mass.

With plutonium, ***the possibility of implosion is very real, and must be avoided at all costs***. This can be accomplished by keeping the various masses separate.

Comments

It's best to avoid using plutonium **at all** if it can be avoided.

Figure 1-7. Using generic and specific selectors to combine styles

In this situation, any warning text will be italicized, but only the text within a span element with a class of warning will be both boldfaced and italicized.

Notice the format of the general class selector in the previous example: it's simply a class name preceded by a period without any element name, and no universal selector. In cases where you only want to select all elements that share a class name, you can omit the universal selector from a class selector without any ill effects.

Multiple Classes

In the previous section, we dealt with class values that contained a single word. In HTML, it's possible to have a space-separated list of words in a single class value. For example, if you want to mark a particular element as being both urgent and a warning, you could write:

```
<p class="urgent warning">When handling plutonium, care must be taken to
avoid the formation of a critical mass.</p>
<p>With plutonium, <span class="warning">the possibility of implosion is
very real, and must be avoided at all costs</span>. This can be accomplished
by keeping the various masses separate.</p>
```

The order of the words doesn't actually matter; `warning urgent` would also suffice and would yield precisely the same results no matter what CSS is written.

Now let's say you want all elements with a `class` of `warning` to be boldfaced, those with a `class` of `urgent` to be italic, and those elements with both values to have a silver background. This would be written as follows:

```
.warning {font-weight: bold;}
.urgent {font-style: italic;}
.warning.urgent {background: silver;}
```

By chaining two class selectors together, you can select only those elements that have both class names, in any order. As you can see, the HTML source contains `class="urgent warning"` but the CSS selector is written `.warning.urgent`. Regardless, the rule will still cause the "When handling plutonium . . . " paragraph to have a silver background, as illustrated in Figure 1-8. This happens because the order the words are written in doesn't matter. (This is not to say the order of classes is always irrelevant, but we'll get to that later in the book.)

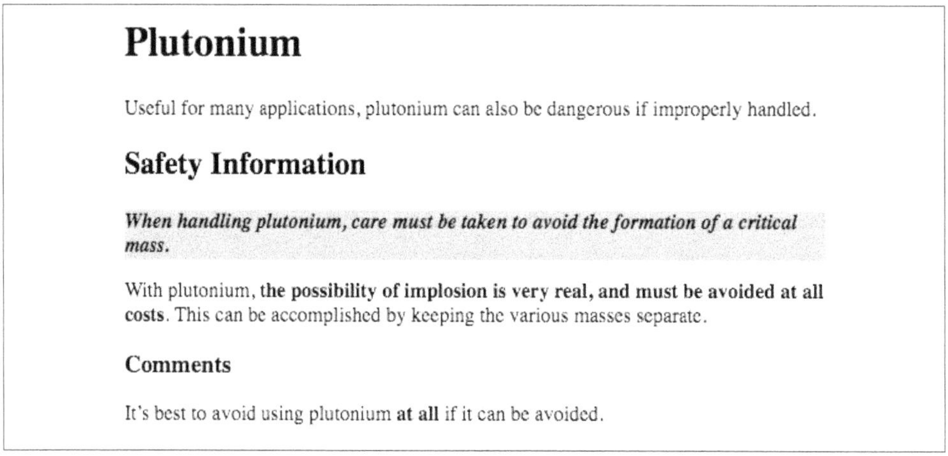

Plutonium

Useful for many applications, plutonium can also be dangerous if improperly handled.

Safety Information

When handling plutonium, care must be taken to avoid the formation of a critical mass.

With plutonium, **the possibility of implosion is very real, and must be avoided at all costs**. This can be accomplished by keeping the various masses separate.

Comments

It's best to avoid using plutonium **at all** if it can be avoided.

Figure 1-8. Selecting elements with multiple class names

If a multiple class selector contains a name that is not in the space-separated list, then the match will fail. Consider the following rule:

```
p.warning.help {background: red;}
```

As you would expect, the selector will match only those p elements with a `class` containing the words `warning` and `help`. Therefore, it will not match a p element with just the words `warning` and `urgent` in its `class` attribute. It would, however, match the following:

```
<p class="urgent warning help">Help me!</p>
```

In versions previous to IE7, Internet Explorer for both platforms has problems with correctly handling multiple class selectors. In these older versions, although you can select a single class name out of a list, selecting based on multiple names in a list does not work properly. Thus, `p.warning` would work as expected, but `p.warning.help` would match any `p` elements that have a `class` attribute with the word `help` because it comes last in the selector. If you wrote `p.help.warning`, then older versions of Explorer would match any `p` elements that have `warning` in their `class` value, whether or not `help` appears in the same value.

ID Selectors

In some ways, ID selectors are similar to class selectors, but there are a few crucial differences. First, ID selectors are preceded by an octothorpe (#)—also known as a pound sign (in the US), hash mark, or tic-tac-toe board—instead of a period. Thus, you might see a rule like this one:

```
*#first-para {font-weight: bold;}
```

This rule produces boldfaced text in any element whose `id` attribute has a value of `first-para`.

The second difference is that instead of referencing values of the `class` attribute, ID selectors refer, unsurprisingly, to values found in `id` attributes. Here's an example of an ID selector in action:

```
*#lead-para {font-weight: bold;}

<p id="lead-para">This paragraph will be boldfaced.</p>
<p>This paragraph will NOT be bold.</p>
```

Note that the value `lead-para` could have been assigned to any element within the document. In this particular case, it is applied to the first paragraph, but you could have applied it just as easily to the second or third paragraph.

As with class selectors, it is possible to omit the universal selector from an ID selector. In the previous example, you could also have written:

```
#lead-para {font-weight: bold;}
```

The effect of this selector would be the same.

Another similarity between classes and IDs is that IDs can also be selected independently of an element. There may be circumstances in which you know that a certain ID value will appear in a document, but you don't know the element on which it will appear (as in the plutonium-handling warnings), so you'll want to declare standalone ID selectors. For example, you may know that in any given document, there will be an element with an ID value of `mostImportant`. You don't know whether that most important thing will be a paragraph, a short phrase, a list item, or a section heading. You know only that it will exist in each document, occur in an arbitrary element, and appear no more than once. In that case, you would write a rule like this:

```
#mostImportant {color: red; background: yellow;}
```

This rule would match any of the following elements (which, as noted before, should *not* appear together in the same document because they all have the same ID value):

```
<h1 id="mostImportant">This is important!</h1>
<em id="mostImportant">This is important!</em>
<ul id="mostImportant">This is important!</ul>
```

Deciding Between Class and ID

You may assign classes to any number of elements, as demonstrated earlier; the class name warning was applied to both a p and a span element, and it could have been applied to many more elements. IDs, on the other hand, are used once, and only once, within an HTML document. Therefore, if you have an element with an id value of lead-para, no other element in that document can have an id value of lead-para.

> In the real world, browsers don't always check for the uniqueness of IDs in HTML. That means that if you sprinkle an HTML document with several elements, all of which have the same value for their ID attributes, you'll probably get the same styles applied to each. This is incorrect behavior, but it happens anyway. Having more than one of the same ID value in a document also makes DOM scripting more difficult, since functions like getElementById() depend on there being one, and only one, element with a given ID value.

Unlike class selectors, ID selectors can't be combined, since ID attributes do not permit a space-separated list of words.

Another difference between class and id names is that IDs carry more weight when you're trying to determine which styles should be applied to a given element. This will be explained in greater detail later on.

Also note that class and ID selectors may be case-sensitive, depending on the document language. HTML defines class and ID values to be case-sensitive, so the capitalization of your class and ID values must match that found in your documents. Thus, in the following pairing of CSS and HTML, the elements text will not be boldfaced:

```
p.criticalInfo {font-weight: bold;}
```

```
<p class="criticalinfo">Don't look down.</p>
```

Because of the change in case for the letter *i*, the selector will not match the element shown.

> Some older browsers did not treat class and ID names as case-sensitive, but all browsers current as of this writing correctly enforce case sensitivity.

On a purely syntactical level, the dot-class notation (e.g., `.warning`) is not guaranteed to work for XML documents. As of this writing, the dot-class notation works in HTML, SVG, and MathML, and it may well be permitted in future languages, but it's up to each language's specification to decide that. The hash-ID notation (e.g., `#lead`) will work in any document language that has an attribute that enforces uniqueness within a document. Uniqueness can be enforced with an attribute called `id`, or indeed anything else, as long as the attribute's contents are defined to be unique within the document.

Attribute Selectors

When it comes to both class and ID selectors, what you're really doing is selecting values of attributes. The syntax used in the previous two sections is particular to HTML, XHTML, SVG, and MathML documents (as of this writing). In other markup languages, these class and ID selectors may not be available (as, indeed, those attributes may not be present). To address this situation, CSS2 introduced *attribute selectors*, which can be used to select elements based on their attributes and the values of those attributes. There are four general types of attribute selectors: simple attribute selectors, exact attribute value selectors, partial-match attribute value selectors, and leading-value attribute selectors.

Simple Attribute Selectors

If you want to select elements that have a certain attribute, regardless of that attribute's value, you can use a simple attribute selector. For example, to select all `h1` elements that have a `class` attribute with any value and make their text silver, write:

```
h1[class] {color: silver;}
```

So, given the following markup:

```
<h1 class="hoopla">Hello</h1>
<h1>Serenity</h1>
<h1 class="fancy">Fooling</h1>
```

...you get the result shown in Figure 1-9.

Figure 1-9. Selecting elements based on their attributes

This strategy is very useful in XML documents, as XML languages tend to have element and attribute names that are very specific to their purpose. Consider an XML language that is used to describe planets of the solar system (we'll call it PlanetML). If you want to select all planet elements with a moons attribute and make them boldface, thus calling attention to any planet that has moons, you would write:

```
planet[moons] {font-weight: bold;}
```

This would cause the text of the second and third elements in the following markup fragment to be boldfaced, but not the first:

```
<planet>Venus</planet>
<planet moons="1">Earth</planet>
<planet moons="2">Mars</planet>
```

In HTML documents, you can use this feature in a number of creative ways. For example, you could style all images that have an alt attribute, thus highlighting those images that are correctly formed:

```
img[alt] {border: 3px solid red;}
```

(This particular example is generally useful more for diagnostic purposes—that is, determining whether images are indeed correctly marked up—than for design purposes.)

If you wanted to boldface any element that includes title information, which most browsers display as a "tool tip" when a cursor hovers over the element, you could write:

```
*[title] {font-weight: bold;}
```

Similarly, you could style only those anchors (a elements) that have an href attribute, thus applying the styles to any hyperlink but not to any named anchors.

It is also possible to select based on the presence of more than one attribute. You do this simply by chaining the attribute selectors together. For example, to boldface the text of any HTML hyperlink that has both an href and a title attribute, you would write:

```
a[href][title] {font-weight: bold;}
```

This would boldface the first link in the following markup, but not the second or third:

```
<a href="http://www.w3.org/" title="W3C Home">W3C</a><br />
<a href="http://www.webstandards.org">Standards Info</a><br />
<a name="dead" title="Not a link">dead.letter</a>
```

Selection Based on Exact Attribute Value

You can further narrow the selection process to encompass only those elements whose attributes are a certain value. For example, let's say you want to boldface any hyperlink that points to a certain document on the web server. This would look something like:

```
a[href="http://www.css-discuss.org/about.html"] {font-weight: bold;}
```

This will boldface the text of any a element that has an href attribute with *exactly* the value *http://www.css-discuss.org/about.html*. Any change at all, even dropping the www. part, will prevent a match.

Any attribute and value combination can be specified for any element. However, if that exact combination does not appear in the document, then the selector won't match anything. Again, XML languages can benefit from this approach to styling. Let's return to our PlanetML example. Suppose you want to select only those planet elements that have a value of 1 for the attribute moons:

```
planet[moons="1"] {font-weight: bold;}
```

This would boldface the text of the second element in the following markup fragment, but not the first or third:

```
<planet>Venus</planet>
<planet moons="1">Earth</planet>
<planet moons="2">Mars</planet>
```

As with attribute selection, you can chain together multiple attribute-value selectors to select a single document. For example, to double the size of the text of any HTML hyperlink that has both an href with a value of *http://www.w3.org/* and a title attribute with a value of W3C Home, you would write:

```
a[href="http://www.w3.org/"][title="W3C Home"] {font-size: 200%;}
```

This would double the text size of the first link in the following markup, but not the second or third:

```
<a href="http://www.w3.org/" title="W3C Home">W3C</a><br />
<a href="http://www.webstandards.org"
   title="Web Standards Organization">Standards Info</a><br />
<a href="http://www.example.org/" title="W3C Home">dead.link</a>
```

The results are shown in Figure 1-10.

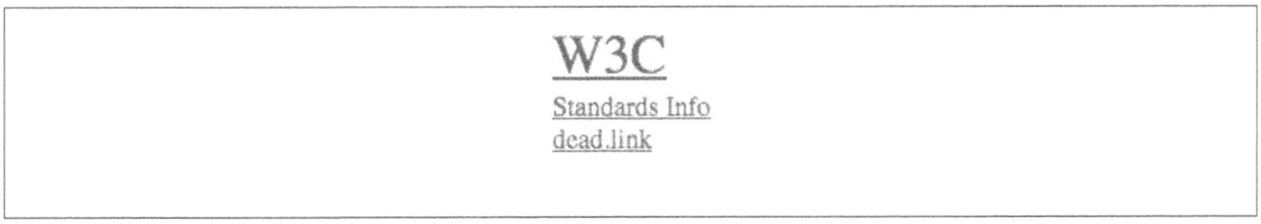

Figure 1-10. Selecting elements based on attributes and their values

Again, this format requires an *exact* match for the attribute's value. Matching becomes an issue when the selector form encounters values that can in turn contain a space-separated list of values (e.g., the HTML attribute class). For example, consider the following markup fragment:

```
<planet type="barren rocky">Mercury</planet>
```

The only way to match this element based on its exact attribute value is to write:

```
planet[type="barren rocky"] {font-weight: bold;}
```

If you were to write planet[type="barren"], the rule would not match the example markup and thus would fail. This is true even for the **class** attribute in HTML. Consider the following:

```
<p class="urgent warning">When handling plutonium, care must be taken to
avoid the formation of a critical mass.</p>
```

To select this element based on its exact attribute value, you would have to write:

```
p[class="urgent warning"] {font-weight: bold;}
```

This is *not* equivalent to the dot-class notation covered earlier, as we will see in the next section. Instead, it selects any p element whose **class** attribute has *exactly* the value **urgent warning**, with the words in that order and a single space between them. It's effectively an exact string match.

Also, be aware that ID selectors and attribute selectors that target the **id** attribute are not precisely the same. In other words, there is a subtle but crucial difference between **h1#page-title** and **h1[id="page-title"]**. This difference is explained in the next chapter in the section on specificity.

Selection Based on Partial Attribute Values

The CSS Selectors Level 3 module, which became a full W3C Recommendation in late 2011, contains a few partial-value attribute selectors—or, as the specification calls them, "substring matching attribute selectors." These are summarized in Table 1-1.

Table 1-1. Substring matching with attribute selectors

Type	Description
[foo~="bar"]	Selects any element with an attribute foo whose value contains the word bar in a space-separated list of words.
[foo*="bar"]	Selects any element with an attribute foo whose value *contains* the substring bar.
[foo^="bar"]	Selects any element with an attribute foo whose value *begins* with bar.
[foo$="bar"]	Selects any element with an attribute foo whose value *ends* with bar.

Matching one word in a space-separated list

For any attribute that accepts a space-separated list of words, it is possible to select elements based on the presence of any one of those words. The classic example in HTML is the **class** attribute, which can accept one or more words as its value. Consider our usual example text:

```
<p class="urgent warning">When handling plutonium, care must be taken to
avoid the formation of a critical mass.</p>
```

Let's say you want to select elements whose **class** attribute contains the word **warning**. You can do this with an attribute selector:

```
p[class~="warning"] {font-weight: bold;}
```

Note the presence of the tilde (~) in the selector. It is the key to selection based on the presence of a space-separated word within the attribute's value. If you omit the tilde, you would have an exact value matching attribute selector, as discussed in the previous section.

This selector construct is equivalent to the dot-class notation discussed earlier in the chapter. Thus, `p.warning` and `p[class~="warning"]` are equivalent when applied to HTML documents. Here's an example that is an HTML version of the "PlanetML" markup seen earlier:

```
<span class="barren rocky">Mercury</span>
<span class="cloudy barren">Venus</span>
<span class="life-bearing cloudy">Earth</span>
```

To italicize all elements with the word `barren` in their `class` attribute, you write:

```
span[class~="barren"] {font-style: italic;}
```

This rule's selector will match the first two elements in the example markup and thus italicize their text, as shown in Figure 1-11. This is the same result we would expect from writing `span.barren {font-style: italic;}`.

Mercury Venus Earth

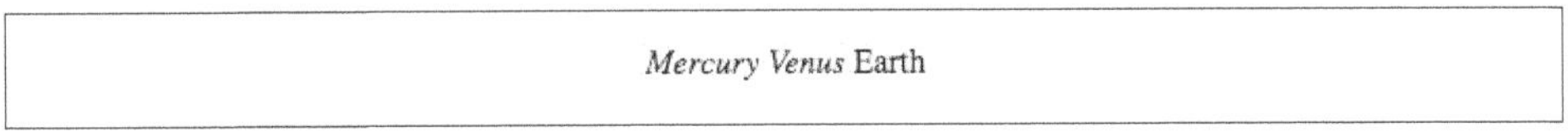

Figure 1-11. Selecting elements based on portions of attribute values

So why bother with the tilde-equals attribute selector in HTML? Because it can be used for any attribute, not just `class`. For example, you might have a document that contains a number of images, only some of which are figures. You can use a partial-match value attribute selector aimed at the `title` text to select only those figures:

```
img[title~="Figure"] {border: 1px solid gray;}
```

This rule will select any image whose `title` text contains the word `Figure`. Therefore, as long as all your figures have `title` text that looks something like "Figure 4. A bald-headed elder statesman," this rule will match those images. For that matter, the selector `img[title~="Figure"]` will also match a title attribute with the value "How to Figure Out Who's in Charge." Any image that does not have a `title` attribute, or whose `title` value doesn't contain the word "Figure," won't be matched.

Matching a substring within an attribute value

Sometimes you want to select elements based on a portion of their attribute values, but the values in question aren't space-separated lists of words. In these cases, you can use the form `[att*="val"]` to match substrings that appear anywhere inside the attribute values. For example, the following CSS matches any `span` element whose `class` attribute contains the substring `cloud`, so both "cloudy" planets are matched, as shown in Figure 1-12.

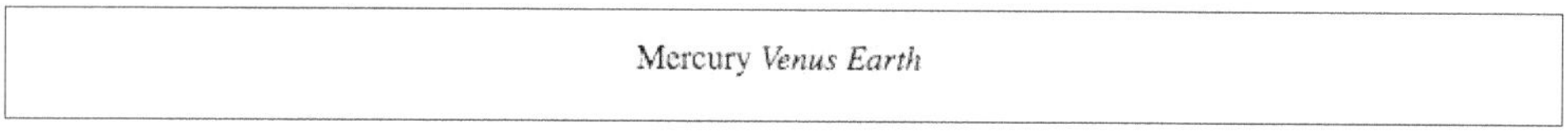

Figure 1-12. Selecting elements based on substrings within attribute values

```
span[class*="cloud"] {font-style: italic;}

<span class="barren rocky">Mercury</span>
<span class="cloudy barren">Venus</span>
<span class="life-bearing cloudy">Earth</span>
```

As you can imagine, there are many useful applications for this particular capability. For example, suppose you wanted to specially style any links to the O'Reilly Media website. Instead of classing them all and writing styles based on that class, you could simply write the following rule:

```
a[href*="oreilly.com"] {font-weight: bold;}
```

Of course, you aren't confined to the `class` and `href` attributes. Any attribute is up for grabs here. `title`, `alt`, `src`, `id`... you name it, you can style based on a substring within an attribute's value. The following rule draws attention to any spacer GIF in an old-school table layout (plus any other image with the string "space" in its source URL):

```
img[src*="space"] {border: 5px solid red;}
```

The matches are exact: if you include whitespace in your selector, then whitespace must also be present in an attribute's value. The attribute names and values must be case-sensitive only if the underlying document language requires case sensitivity.

Matching a substring at the beginning of an attribute value

In cases where you want to select elements based on a substring at the beginning of an attribute value, then the attribute selector pattern `[att^="val"]` is what you're seeking. This can be particularly useful in a situation where you want to style types of links differently, as illustrated in Figure 1-13.

```
a[href^="https:"] {font-weight: bold;}
a[href^="mailto:"] {font-style: italic;}
```

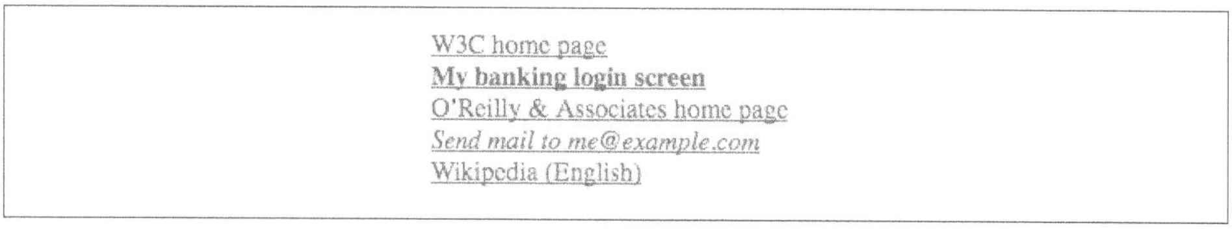

> W3C home page
> **My banking login screen**
> O'Reilly & Associates home page
> *Send mail to me@example.com*
> Wikipedia (English)

Figure 1-13. Selecting elements based on substrings that begin attribute values

Another use case is when you want to style all images in an article that are also figures, as in the figures you see throughout this text. Assuming that the alt text of each figure begins with text in the pattern "Figure 5"—which is an entirely reasonable assumption in this case—then you can select only those images as follows:

```
img[alt^="Figure"] {border: 2px solid gray;  display: block; margin: 2em auto;}
```

The potential drawback here is that *any* img element whose alt starts with "Figure" will be selected, whether or not it's meant to be an illustrative figure. The likeliness of that occurring depends on the document in question, obviously.

One more use case is selecting all of the calendar events that occur on Mondays. In this case, all of the events have a title attribute containing a date in the format "Monday, March 5th, 2012." Selecting them all is a simple matter of [title^="Monday"].

Matching a substring at the end of an attribute value

The mirror image of beginning-substring matching is ending-substring matching, which is accomplished using the [att$="val"] pattern. A very common use for this capability is to style links based on the kind of resource they target, such as separate styles for PDF documents, as illustrated in Figure 1-14.

```
a[href$=".pdf"] {font-weight: bold;}
```

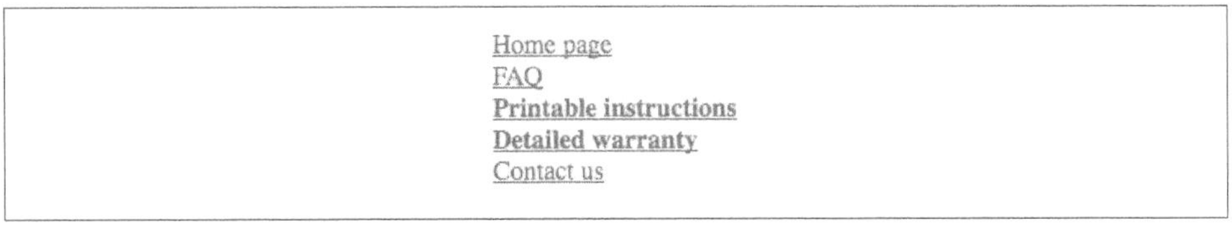

Home page
FAQ
Printable instructions
Detailed warranty
Contact us

Figure 1-14. Selecting elements based on substrings that end attribute values

Similarly, you could (for whatever reason) select images based on their image format:

```
img[src$=".gif"] {...}
img[src$=".jpg"] {...}
img[src$=".png"] {...}
```

To continue the calendar example from the previous section, it would be possible to select all of the events occurring within a given year using a selector like [title $="2012"].

A Particular Attribute Selection Type

The last type of attribute selector, the particular attribute selector, is easier to show than it is to describe. Consider the following rule:

```
*[lang|="en"] {color: white;}
```

This rule will select any element whose lang attribute is equal to en or begins with en-. Therefore, the first three elements in the following example markup would be selected, but the last two would not:

```
<h1 lang="en">Hello!</h1>
<p lang="en-us">Greetings!</p>
<div lang="en-au">G'day!</div>
```

```
<p lang="fr">Bonjour!</p>
<h4 lang="cy-en">Jrooana!</h4>
```

In general, the form [att|="val"] can be used for any attribute and its values. Let's say you have a series of figures in an HTML document, each of which has a filename like *figure-1.gif* and *figure-3.jpg*. You can match all of these images using the following selector:

```
img[src|="figure"] {border: 1px solid gray;}
```

The most common use for this type of attribute selector is to match language values, as demonstrated later in this chapter.

Using Document Structure

As mentioned previously, CSS is powerful because it uses the structure of documents to determine appropriate styles and how to apply them. That's only part of the story since it implies that such determinations are the only way CSS uses document structure. Structure plays a much larger role in the way styles are applied to a document. Let's take a moment to discuss structure before moving on to more powerful forms of selection.

Understanding the Parent-Child Relationship

To understand the relationship between selectors and documents, you need to once again examine how documents are structured. Consider this very simple HTML document:

```
<html>
<head>
 <base href="http://www.meerkat.web/">
 <title>Meerkat Central</title>
</head>
<body>
 <h1>Meerkat <em>Central</em></h1>
 <p>
 Welcome to Meerkat <em>Central</em>, the <strong>best meerkat web site
 on <a href="inet.html">the <em>entire</em> Internet</a></strong>!</p>
 <ul>
  <li>We offer:
   <ul>
    <li><strong>Detailed information</strong> on how to adopt a meerkat</li>
    <li>Tips for living with a meerkat</li>
    <li><em>Fun</em> things to do with a meerkat, including:
     <ol>
      <li>Playing fetch</li>
      <li>Digging for food</li>
      <li>Hide and seek</li>
     </ol>
    </li>
   </ul>
 </ul>
```

```
    </li>
    <li>...and so much more!</li>
    </ul>
    <p>
    Questions? <a href="mailto:suricate@meerkat.web">Contact us!</a>
    </p>
    </body>
    </html>
```

Much of the power of CSS is based on the *parent-child relationship* of elements. HTML documents (actually, most structured documents of any kind) are based on a hierarchy of elements, which is visible in the "tree" view of the document (see Figure 1-15). In this hierarchy, each element fits somewhere into the overall structure of the document. Every element in the document is either the *parent* or the *child* of another element, and it's often both.

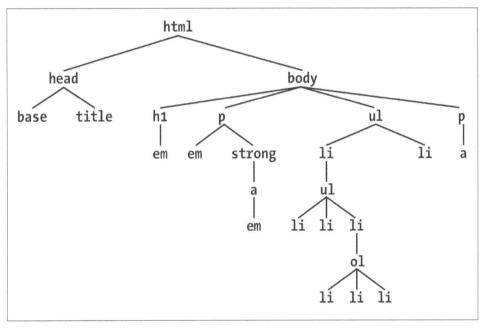

Figure 1-15. A document tree structure

An element is said to be the parent of another element if it appears directly above that element in the document hierarchy. For example, in Figure 1-15, the first p element is parent to the em and strong elements, while strong is parent to an anchor (a) element, which is itself parent to another em element. Conversely, an element is the child of another element if it is directly beneath the other element. Thus, the anchor element in Figure 1-15 is a child of the strong element, which is in turn child to the p element, and so on.

The terms "parent" and "child" are specific applications of the terms *ancestor* and *descendant*. There is a difference between them: in the tree view, if an element is exactly one level above another, then they have a parent-child relationship. If the path from one element to another is traced through two or more levels, the elements have an ancestor-descendant relationship, but not a parent-child relationship. (Of course, a child is also a descendant, and a parent is an ancestor.) In Figure 1-15, the first ul element is parent to two li elements, but the first ul is also the ancestor of every element descended from its li element, all the way down to the most deeply nested li elements.

Also, in Figure 1-15, there is an anchor that is a child of strong, but also a descendant of paragraph, body, and html elements. The body element is an ancestor of everything that the browser will display by default, and the html element is ancestor to the entire document. For this reason, the html element is also called the *root element*.

Descendant Selectors

The first benefit of understanding this model is the ability to define *descendant selectors* (also known as *contextual selectors*). Defining descendant selectors is the act of creating rules that operate in certain structural circumstances but not others. As an example, let's say you want to style only those em elements that are descended from h1 elements. You could put a class attribute on every em element found within an h1, but that's almost as time-consuming as using the font tag. It's obviously far more efficient to declare rules that match only em elements that are found inside h1 elements.

To do so, write the following:

```
h1 em {color: gray;}
```

This rule will make gray any text in an em element that is the descendant of an h1 element. Other em text, such as that found in a paragraph or a block quote, will not be selected by this rule. Figure 1-16 makes this clear.

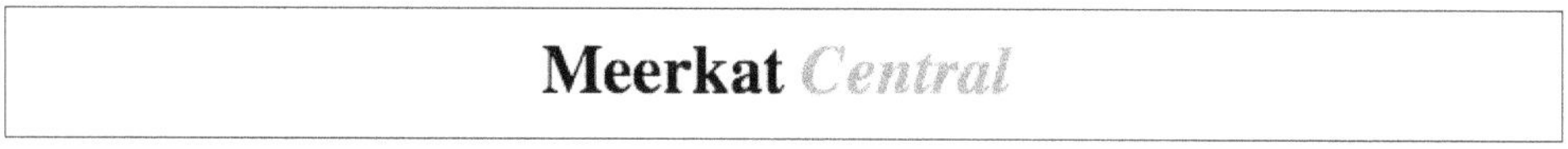

Figure 1-16. Selecting an element based on its context

In a descendant selector, the selector side of a rule is composed of two or more space-separated selectors. The space between the selectors is an example of a *combinator*. Each space combinator can be translated as "found within," "which is part of," or "that is a descendant of," but only if you read the selector right to left. Thus, h1 em can be translated as, "Any em element that is a descendant of an h1 element." (To read the selector left to right, you might phrase it something like, "Any h1 that contains an em will have the following styles applied to the em.")

You aren't limited to two selectors, of course. For example:

```
ul ol ul em {color: gray;}
```

In this case, as Figure 1-17 shows, any emphasized text that is part of an unordered list that is part of an ordered list that is itself part of an unordered list (yes, this is correct) will be gray. This is obviously a very specific selection criterion.

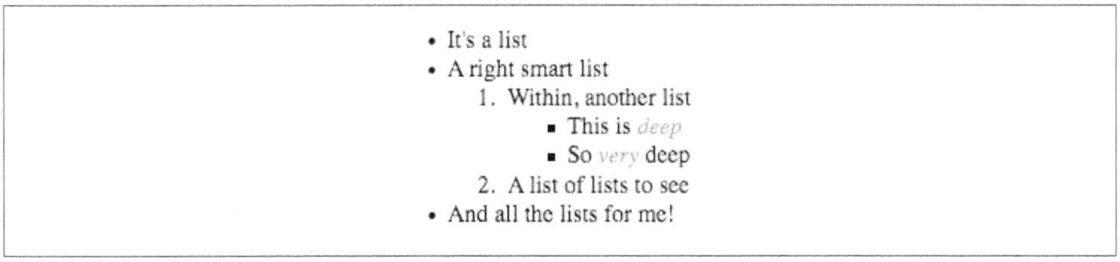

- It's a list
- A right smart list
    1. Within, another list
        - This is *deep*
        - So *very* deep
    2. A list of lists to see
- And all the lists for me!

Figure 1-17. A very specific descendant selector

Descendant selectors can be extremely powerful. They make possible what could never be done in HTML—at least not without oodles of font tags. Let's consider a common example. Assume you have a document with a sidebar and a main area. The sidebar has a blue background, the main area has a white background, and both areas include lists of links. You can't set all links to be blue because they'd be impossible to read in the sidebar.

The solution: descendant selectors. In this case, you give the element (probably a div) that contains your sidebar a class of `sidebar`, and assign the main area a class of `main`. Then, you write styles like this:

```
.sidebar {background: blue;}
.main {background: white;}
.sidebar a:link {color: white;}
.main a:link {color: blue;}
```

Figure 1-18 shows the result.

Blogs

These are the web logs ("blogs") I visit a lot. They're all written by people who know a lot about Web design and CSS in general. By reading them I can get a sense of the trends in design and thinking about document structure.

css-tricks.com
lea.verou.me
meyerweb.com
tantek.com
zeldman.com

Figure 1-18. Using descendant selectors to apply different styles to the same type of element

 :link refers to links to resources that haven't been visited. We'll talk about it in detail later in this chapter.

Here's another example: let's say that you want gray to be the text color of any b (bold-face) element that is part of a blockquote, and also for any bold text that is found in a normal paragraph:

```
blockquote b, p b {color: gray;}
```

The result is that the text within b elements that are descended from paragraphs or block quotes will be gray.

One overlooked aspect of descendant selectors is that the degree of separation between two elements can be practically infinite. For example, if you write ul em, that syntax will select any em element descended from a ul element, no matter how deeply nested the em may be. Thus, ul em would select the em element in the following markup:

```
<ul>
<li>List item 1
<ol>
<li>List item 1-1</li>
<li>List item 1-2</li>
<li>List item 1-3
<ol>
<li>List item 1-3-1</li>
<li>List item <em>1-3-2</em></li>
<li>List item 1-3-3</li>
</ol></li>
<li>List item 1-4</li>
</ol></li>
</ul>
```

Another, even subtler aspect of descendant selectors is that they have no notion of element proximity. In other words, the closeness of two elements within the document tree has no bearing on whether a rule applies or not. This has bearing when it comes to specificity (which we'll cover later on) but also when considering rules that might appear to cancel each other out.

For example, consider the following (which contains a selector type we'll discuss later in this chapter):

```
div:not(.help) span {color: gray;}
div.help span {color: red;}

<div class="help">
    <div class="aside">
        This text contains <span>a span element</span> within.
    </div>
</div>
```

What the CSS says, in effect, is "any span inside a div that doesn't have a class containing the word help should be gray" in the first rule, and "any span inside a div whose class contains the word help" in the second rule. In the given markup fragment, *both* rules apply to the span shown.

Because the two rules have equal weight and the "red" rule is written last, it wins out and the span is red. The fact that the div class="aside" is "closer to" the span than the div class="help" is completely irrelevant. Again: descendant selectors have no notion of element proximity. Both rules match, only one color can be applied, and due to the way CSS works, red is the winner here.

Selecting Children

In some cases, you don't want to select an arbitrarily descended element; rather, you want to narrow your range to select an element that is a child of another element. You might, for example, want to select a strong element only if it is a child (as opposed to any level of descendant) of an h1 element. To do this, you use the child combinator, which is the greater-than symbol (>):

```
h1 > strong {color: red;}
```

This rule will make red the strong element shown in the first h1 below, but not the second:

```
<h1>This is <strong>very</strong> important.</h1>
<h1>This is <em>really <strong>very</strong></em> important.</h1>
```

Read right to left, the selector h1 > strong translates as, "Selects any strong element that is a child of an h1 element." The child combinator can be optionally surrounded by whitespace. Thus, h1 > strong, h1> strong, and h1>strong are all equivalent. You can use or omit whitespace as you wish.

When viewing the document as a tree structure, it's easy to see that a child selector restricts its matches to elements that are directly connected in the tree. Figure 1-19 shows part of a document tree.

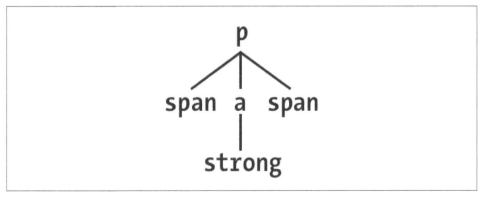

Figure 1-19. A document tree fragment

In this tree fragment, you can easily pick out parent-child relationships. For example, the a element is parent to the strong, but it is child to the p element. You could match elements in this fragment with the selectors `p > a` and `a > strong`, but not `p > strong`, since the `strong` is a descendant of the `p` but not its child.

You can also combine descendant and child combinations in the same selector. Thus, `table.summary td > p` will select any `p` element that is a child of a `td` element that is itself descended from a `table` element that has a `class` attribute containing the word `summary`.

Selecting Adjacent Sibling Elements

Let's say you want to style the paragraph immediately after a heading or give a special margin to a list that immediately follows a paragraph. To select an element that immediately follows another element with the same parent, you use the *adjacent-sibling combinator*, represented as a plus symbol (+). As with the child combinator, the symbol can be surrounded by whitespace, or not, at the author's discretion.

To remove the top margin from a paragraph immediately following an `h1` element, write:

```
h1 + p {margin-top: 0;}
```

The selector is read as, "Selects any `p` element that immediately follows an `h1` element that shares a parent with the `p` element."

To visualize how this selector works, it is easiest to once again consider a fragment of a document tree, shown in Figure 1-20.

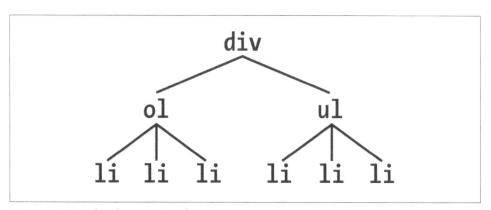

Figure 1-20. Another document tree fragment

In this fragment, a pair of lists descends from a `div` element, one ordered and the other not, each containing three list items. Each list is an adjacent sibling, and the list items themselves are also adjacent siblings. However, the list items from the first list are *not* siblings of the second, since the two sets of list items do not share the same parent element. (At best, they're cousins, and CSS has no cousin selector.)

Remember that you can select the second of two adjacent siblings only with a single combinator. Thus, if you write `li + li {font-weight: bold;}`, only the second and third items in each list will be boldfaced. The first list items will be unaffected, as illustrated in Figure 1-21.

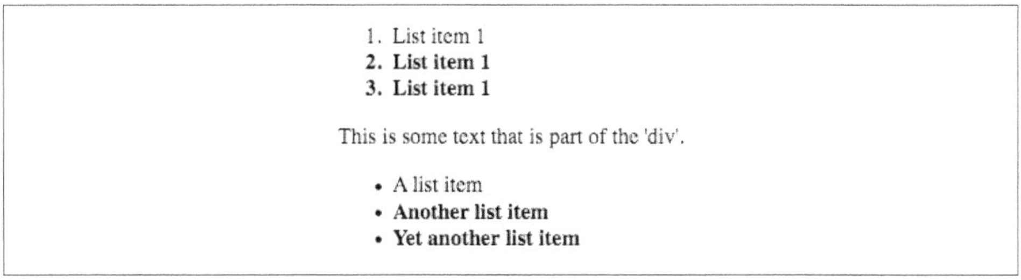

1. List item 1
2. **List item 1**
3. **List item 1**

This is some text that is part of the 'div'.

- A list item
- **Another list item**
- **Yet another list item**

Figure 1-21. Selecting adjacent siblings

To work properly, CSS requires that the two elements appear in "source order." In our example, an `ol` element is followed by a `ul` element. This allows you to select the second element with `ol + ul`, but you cannot select the first using the same syntax. For `ul + ol` to match, an ordered list must immediately follow an unordered list.

Keep in mind that text content between two elements does *not* prevent the adjacent-sibling combinator from working. Consider this markup fragment, whose tree view would be the same as that shown in Figure 1-19:

```
<div>
<ol>
<li>List item 1</li>
<li>List item 1</li>
<li>List item 1</li>
</ol>
This is some text that is part of the 'div'.
<ul>
<li>A list item</li>
<li>Another list item</li>
<li>Yet another list item</li>
</ul>
</div>
```

Even though there is text between the two lists, you can still match the second list with the selector `ol + ul`. That's because the intervening text is not contained with a sibling element, but is instead part of the parent `div`. If you wrapped that text in a paragraph element, it would then prevent `ol + ul` from matching the second list. Instead, you might have to write something like `ol + p + ul`.

As the following example illustrates, the adjacent-sibling combinator can be used in conjunction with other combinators:

```
html > body table + ul{margin-top: 1.5em;}
```

The selector translates as, "Selects any ul element that immediately follows a sibling table element that is descended from a body element that is itself a child of an html element."

As with all combinators, you can place the adjacent-sibling combinator in a more complex setting, such as div#content h1 + div ol. That selector is read as, "Selects any ol element that is descended from a div when the div is the adjacent sibling of an h1 which is itself descended from a div whose id attribute has a value of content."

Selecting Following Siblings

Selectors Level 3 introduced a new sibling combinator called the *general sibling combinator*. This lets you select any element that follows another element when both elements share the same parent, represented using the tilde (~) combinator.

As an example, to italicize any ol that follows an h2 and also shares a parent with the h2, you'd write h2 ~ ol {font-style: italic;}. The two elements do not have to be adjacent siblings, although they can be adjacent and still match this rule. The result of applying this rule to the following markup is shown in Figure 1-22.

```
<div>
<h2>Subheadings</h2>
<p>It is the case that not every heading can be a main heading.  Some headings must be
subheadings.  Examples include:</p>
<ol>
<li>Headings that are less important</li>
<li>Headings that are subsidiary to more important headlines</li>
<li>Headings that like to be dominated</li>
</ol>
<p>Let's restate that for the record:</p>
<ol>
<li>Headings that are less important</li>
<li>Headings that are subsidiary to more important headlines</li>
<li>Headings that like to be dominated</li>
</ol>
</div>
```

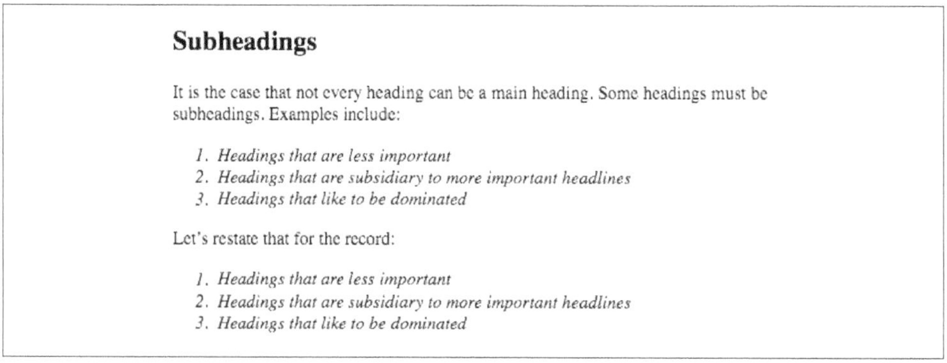

Figure 1-22. Selecting following siblings

As you can see, both ordered lists are italicized. That's because both of them are ol elements that follow an h2 with whom they share a parent (the div).

Pseudo-Class Selectors

Things get really interesting with *pseudo-class selectors*. These selectors let you assign styles to what are, in effect, phantom classes that are inferred by the state of certain elements, or markup patterns within the document, or even by the state of the document itself.

The phrase "phantom classes" might seem a little odd, but it really is the best way to think of how pseudo-classes work. For example, suppose you wanted to highlight every other row of a data table. You could do that by marking up every other row something like class="even" and then writing CSS to highlight rows with that class—or (as we'll soon see) you could use a pseudo-class selector to achieve exactly the same effect, and through very similar means.

Combining Pseudo-Classes

Before we start, a word about chaining. CSS makes it possible to combine ("chain") pseudo-classes together. For example, you can make unvisited links red when they're hovered, but visited links maroon when *they're* hovered:

```
a:link:hover {color: red;}
a:visited:hover {color: maroon;}
```

The order you specify doesn't actually matter; you could also write a:hover:link to the same effect as a:link:hover. It's also possible to assign separate hover styles to unvisited and visited links that are in another language—for example, German:

```
a:link:hover:lang(de) {color: gray;}
a:visited:hover:lang(de) {color: silver;}
```

Be careful not to combine mutually exclusive pseudo-classes. For example, a link cannot be both visited and unvisited, so a:link:visited doesn't make any sense. User agents will most likely ignore such a selector and thus effectively ignore the entire rule, although this cannot be guaranteed, as different browsers will have different error-handling behaviors.

Structural Pseudo-Classes

Thanks to Selectors Level 3, the majority of pseudo-classes are structural in nature; that is, they refer to the markup structure of the document. Most of them depend on patterns within the markup, such as choosing every third paragraph, but others allow you to address specific types of elements. All pseudo-classes, without exception, are a word preceded by a single colon (:), and they can appear anywhere in a selector.

Before we get started, there's an aspect of pseudo-classes that needs to be made explicit here: pseudo-classes always refer to the element to which they're attached, and no other. Seems like a weirdly obvious thing to say, right? The reason to make it explicit is that for a few of the structural pseudo-classes in particular, it's a common error to think they are descriptors that refer to descendant elements.

To illustrate this, I'd like to share a personal anecdote. When my eldest daughter, also my first child, was born in 2003, I announced it online (like you do). A number of people responded with congratulations and CSS jokes, chief among them the selector `#ericmeyer:first-child`. The problem there is that selector would select me, and then only if I were the first child of my parents (which, as it happens. I am). To properly select my first child, that selector would need to be `#ericmeyer > :first-child`.

The confusion is understandable, which is why we're addressing it here; reminders will be found throughout the following sections. Just always keep in mind that the effect of pseudo-classes is to apply a sort of a "phantom class" to the element to which they're attached, and you should be okay.

Selecting the root element

This is the quintessence of structural simplicity: the pseudo-class `:root` selects the root element of the document. In HTML, this is *always* the `html` element. The real benefit of this selector is found when writing style sheets for XML languages, where the root element may be different in every language—for example, in RSS 2.0 it's the `rss` element—or even when you have more than one possible root element within a single language (though not, of course, a single document!).

Here's an example of styling the root element in HTML, as illustrated in Figure 1-23:

```
:root {border: 10px dotted gray;}
body {border: 10px solid black;}
```

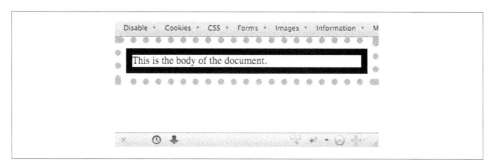

Figure 1-23. Styling the root element

Of course, in HTML documents you can always select the `html` element directly, without having to use the `:root` pseudo-class. There is a difference between the two selectors in terms of specificity, which we'll cover later on.

Selecting empty elements

With the pseudo-class `:empty`, you can select any element that has no children of any kind, *including* text nodes, which covers both text and whitespace. This can be useful in suppressing elements that a CMS has generated without filling in any actual content. Thus, `p:empty {display: none;}` would prevent the display of any empty paragraphs.

Note that in order to be matched, an element must be, from a parsing perspective, truly empty—no whitespace, visible content, or descendant elements. Of the following elements, only the first and last would be matched by `p:empty`.

```
<p></p>
<p> </p>
<p>
</p>
<p><!--a comment--></p>
```

The second and third paragraphs are not matched by `:empty` because they are not empty: they contain, respectively, a single space and a single newline character. Both are considered text nodes, and thus prevent a state of emptiness. The last paragraph matches because comments are not considered content, not even whitespace. But put even one space or newline to either side of that comment, and `p:empty` would fail to match.

You might be tempted to just style all empty elements with something like `*:empty {display: none;}`, but there's a hidden catch: `:empty` matches HTML's empty elements, like `img` and `input`. It could even match `textarea`, unless of course you insert some default text into the `textarea` element. Thus, in terms of matching elements, `img` and `img:empty` are effectively the same. (They are different in terms of specificity, which we'll cover in just a bit.)

As of early 2012, `:empty` is unique in that it's the only CSS selector that takes text nodes into consideration when determining matches. Every other selector type in Selectors Level 3 considers only elements and ignores text nodes entirely—recall, for example, the sibling combinators discussed previously.

Selecting unique children

If you've ever wanted to select all the images that are wrapped by a hyperlink element, the `:only-child` pseudo-class is for you. It selects elements when they are the only child element of another element. So let's say you want to remove the border from any image that's the only child of another element. You'd write:

```
img:only-child {border: 0;}
```

This would match any image that meets those criteria, of course. Therefore, if you had a paragraph which contained an image and no other child elements, the image would be selected regardless of all the text surrounding it. If what you're really after is images that are sole children and found inside hyperlinks, then you just modify the selector like so (which is illustrated in Figure 1-24):

```
a[href] img:only-child {border: 2px solid black;}

<a href="http://w3.org/"><img src="w3.png" alt="W3C"></a>
<a href="http://w3.org/"><img src="w3.png" alt=""> The W3C</a>
<a href="http://w3.org/"><img src="w3.png" alt=""> <em>The W3C</em></a>
```

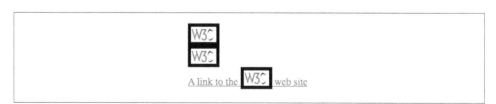

Figure 1-24. Selecting images that are only children inside links

There are two things to remember about :only-child. The first is that you *always* apply it to the element you want to be an only child, not to the parent element, as explained earlier. And that brings up the second thing to remember, which is that when you use :only-child in a descendant selector, you aren't restricting the elements listed to a parent-child relationship. To go back to the hyperlinked-image example, a[href] img:only-child matches any image that is an only child and is descended from an a element, not is a child of an a element. Therefore all three of the images here would be matched, as shown in Figure 1-25.

```
a[href] img:only-child {border: 5px solid black;}

<a href="http://w3.org/"><img src="w3.png" alt="W3C"></a>
<a href="http://w3.org/"><span><img src="w3.png" alt="W3C"></span></a>
<a href="http://w3.org/">A link to <span>the <img src="w3.png" alt=""> web</span>
site</a>
```

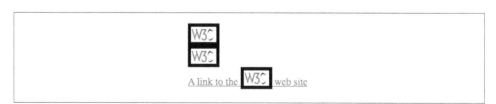

Figure 1-25. Selecting images that are only children inside links

In each case, the image is the only child element of its parent, and it is also descended from an a element. Thus all three images are matched by the rule shown. If you wanted to restrict the rule so that it matched images that were the only children of a elements, then you'd simply add the child combinator to yield a[href] > img:only-child. With that change, only the first of the three images shown in Figure 1-25 would be matched.

That's all great, but what if you want to match images that are the only images inside hyperlinks, but there are other elements in there with them? Consider the following:

```
<a href="http://w3.org/"><b>•</b><img src="w3.png" alt="W3C"></a>
```

In this case, we have an a element that has two children: a b and an img. That image, no longer being the only child of its parent (the hyperlink), can never be matched using :only-child. However, it *can* be matched using :only-of-type. This is illustrated in Figure 1-26.

```
a[href] img:only-of-type {border: 5px solid black;}
```

```
<a href="http://w3.org/"><b>•</b><img src="w3.png" alt="W3C"></a>
<a href="http://w3.org/"><span><b>•</b><img src="w3.png" alt="W3C"></span></a>
```

Figure 1-26. Selecting images that are the only sibling of their type

The difference is that :only-of-type will match any element that is the only of its type among all its siblings, whereas :only-child will only match if an element has no siblings at all.

This can be very useful in cases such as selecting images within paragraphs without having to worry about the presence of hyperlinks or other inline elements:

```
p > img:only-of-type {float: right; margin: 20px;}
```

As long as there aren't multiple images that are children of a paragraph, then the image will be floated. You could also use this pseudo-class to apply extra styles to an h2 when it's the only one in a section of a document.

```
section > h2 {margin: 1em 0 0.33em; font-size: 180%; border-bottom: 1px solid gray;}
section > h2:only-of-type {font-size: 240%;}
```

Given those rules, any section that has only one child h2 will have it appear larger than usual. If there are two or more h2 children to a section, neither of them will be larger than the other. The presence of other children—whether they are other heading levels, paragraphs, tables, paragraphs, lists, and so on—will not interfere with matching.

Selecting first and last children

It's pretty common to want to apply special styling to the first or last children of an element. The most common example is styling a bunch of navigation links into a tab bar, and wanting to put some special visual touches on the first or last tabs (or both). In the past, this was done by applying special classes to those elements. Now we have pseudo-classes to carry the load for us.

The pseudo-class `:first-child` is used to select elements that are the first children of other elements. Consider the following markup:

```
<div>
<p>These are the necessary steps:</p>
<ul>
<li>Insert key</li>
<li>Turn key <strong>clockwise</strong></li>
<li>Push accelerator</li>
</ul>
<p>
Do <em>not</em> push the brake at the same time as the accelerator.
</p>
</div>
```

In this example, the elements that are first children are the first p, the first li, and the strong and em elements. Given the following two rules:

```
p:first-child {font-weight: bold;}
li:first-child {text-transform: uppercase;}
```

...you get the result shown in Figure 1-27.

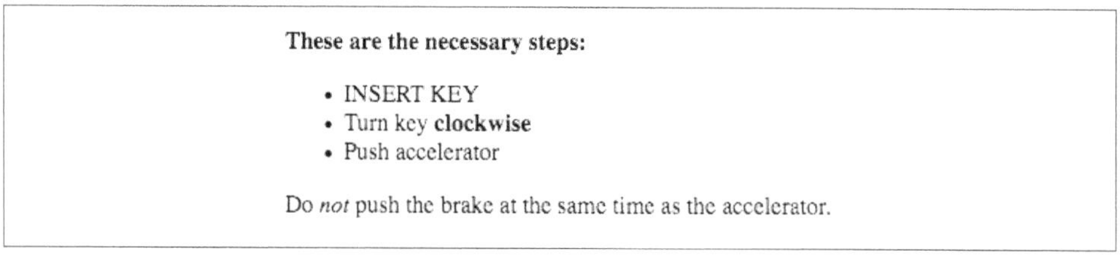

Figure 1-27. Styling first children

The first rule boldfaces any p element that is the first child of another element. The second rule uppercases any li element that is the first child of another element (which, in HTML, must be either an ol or ul element).

As has been mentioned, the most common error is assuming that a selector like `p:first-child` will select the first child of a p element. However, remember the nature of pseudo-classes, which is to attach a sort of phantom class to the element associated with the pseudo-class. If you were to add actual classes to the markup, it would look like this:

```
<div>
<p class="first-child">These are the necessary steps:</p>
<ul>
<li class="first-child">Insert key</li>
<li>Turn key <strong class="first-child">clockwise</strong></li>
<li>Push accelerator</li>
</ul>
<p>
Do <em class="first-child">not</em> push the brake at the same time as the
accelerator.
</p>
</div>
```

Therefore, if you want to select those em elements that are the first child of another element, you write em:first-child.

The mirror image of :first-child is :last-child. If we take the previous example and just change the pseudo-classes, we get the result shown in Figure 1-28.

```
p:last-child {font-weight: bold;}
li:last-child {text-transform: uppercase;}

<div>
<p>These are the necessary steps:</p>
<ul>
<li>Insert key</li>
<li>Turn key <strong>clockwise</strong></li>
<li>Push accelerator</li>
</ul>
<p>
Do <em>not</em> push the brake at the same time as the accelerator.
</p>
</div>
```

These are the necessary steps:

- Insert key
- Turn key **clockwise**
- PUSH ACCELERATOR

Do *not* push the brake at the same time as the accelerator.

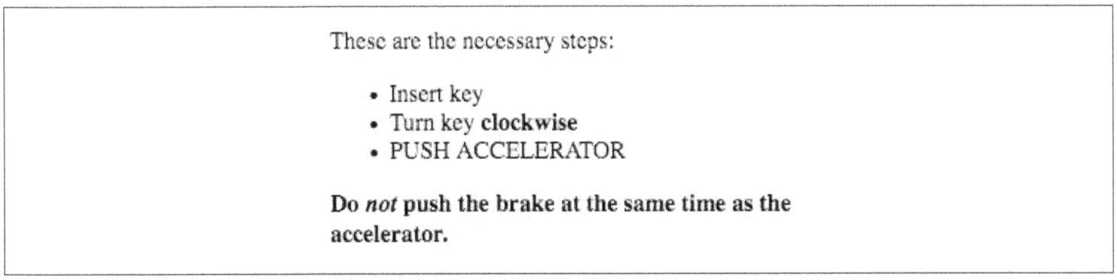

Figure 1-28. Styling last children

The first rule boldfaces any p element that is the last child of another element. The second rule uppercases any li element that is the last child of another element. If you wanted to select the em element inside that last paragraph, you could use the selector p:last-child em, which selects any em element that descends from a p element that is itself the last child of another element.

Interestingly, you can combine these two pseudo-classes to create a version of :only-child. The following two rules will select the same elements:

```
p:only-child {color: red;}
p:first-child:last-child {background: red;}
```

Either way, you'd get paragraphs with red foreground and background colors (not a good idea, clearly). The only difference is in terms of specificity, which we'll cover later in this book.

Selecting first and last of a type

In a manner similar to selecting the first and last children of an element, you can select the first or last of a type of element within an element. This permits things like selecting the first `table` inside a given element, regardless of whatever other elements come before it.

```
table:first-of-type {border-top: 2px solid gray;}
```

Note that this does *not* apply to the entire document; that is, the rule shown will not select the first table in the document and skip all the others. It will instead select the first `table` element within each element that contains one, and skip any sibling `table` elements that come after the first. Thus, given the document structure shown in Figure 1-29, the circled nodes are the ones that are selected.

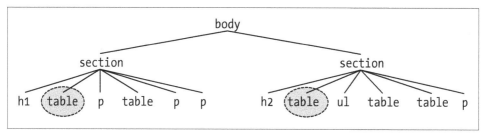

Figure 1-29. Selecting first-of-type tables

Within the context of tables, a useful way to select the first data cell within a row regardless of whether a header cell comes before it in the row is as follows:

```
td:first-of-type {border-left: 1px solid red;}
```

That would select the first data cell in each of the following table rows:

```
<tr><th scope="row">Count</th><td>7</td><td>6</td><td>11</td></tr>
<tr><td>Q</td><td>X</td><td>-</td></tr>
```

Compare that to the effects of `td:first-child`, which would select the first `td` element second row shown, but not in the first row.

The flip side is `:last-of-type`, which selects the last instance of a given type from amongst its sibling elements. In a way, it's just like `:first-of-type` except you start with the last element in a group of siblings and walk backwards toward the first element until you reach an instance of the type. Given the document structure shown in Figure 1-30, the circled nodes are the ones selected by `table:last-of-type`.

As was noted with `:only-of-type`, remember that you are selecting elements of a type from among their sibling elements; thus, every set of siblings is considered separately. In other words, you are *not* selecting the first (or last) of all the elements of a type within the entire document as a single group. Each set of elements that share a parent is its own group, and you can select the first (or last) of a type within each group.

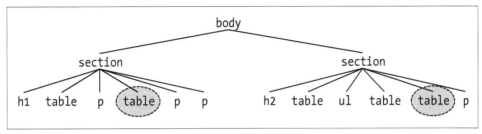

Figure 1-30. Selecting last-of-type tables

Similar to what was noted in the previous section, you can combine these two pseudo-classes to create a version of :only-of-type. The following two rules will select the same elements:

```
table:only-of-type{color: red;}
table:first-of-type:last-of-type {background: red;}
```

Selecting every nth child

If you can select elements that are the first, last, or only children of other elements, how about second children? Third children? Ninth children? Rather than define a literally infinite number of named pseudo-classes, CSS has the :nth-child() pseudo-class. By filling integers or even simple algebraic expressions into the parentheses, you can select any arbitrarily numbered child element you like.

Let's start with the :nth-child() equivalent of :first-child, which is :nth-child(1). In the following example, the selected elements will be the first paragraph and the first list item.

```
p:nth-child(1) {font-weight: bold;}
li:nth-child(1) {text-transform: uppercase;}

<div>
<p>These are the necessary steps:</p>
<ul>
<li>Insert key</li>
<li>Turn key <strong>clockwise</strong></li>
<li>Push accelerator</li>
</ul>
<p>
Do <em>not</em> push the brake at the same time as the accelerator.
</p>
</div>
```

If we were to change the numbers from 1 to 2, however, then no paragraphs would be selected, and the middle list item would be selected, as illustrated in Figure 1-31.

```
p:nth-child(2) {font-weight: bold;}
li:nth-child(2) {text-transform: uppercase;}
```

You can of course insert any integer your choose; if you have a use case for selecting any ordered list that is the 93rd child element of its parent, then ol:nth-child(93) is

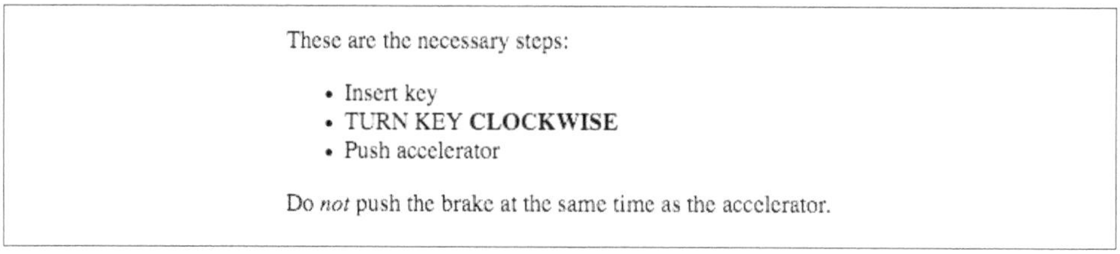

These are the necessary steps:

- Insert key
- TURN KEY **CLOCKWISE**
- Push accelerator

Do *not* push the brake at the same time as the accelerator.

Figure 1-31. Styling second children

ready to serve. (This does not mean the 93rd ordered list among its siblings; see the next section for that.)

More powerfully, you can use simple algebraic expressions in the form *an* + *b* or *an* - *b* to define recurring instances, where *a* and *b* are integers and n is present as itself. Furthermore, the + *b* or - *b* part is optional and thus can be dropped if it isn't needed.

Let's suppose we want to select every third list item in an unordered list, starting with the first. The following makes that possible, as shown in Figure 1-32.

```
ul > li:nth-child(3n + 1) {text-transform: uppercase;}
```

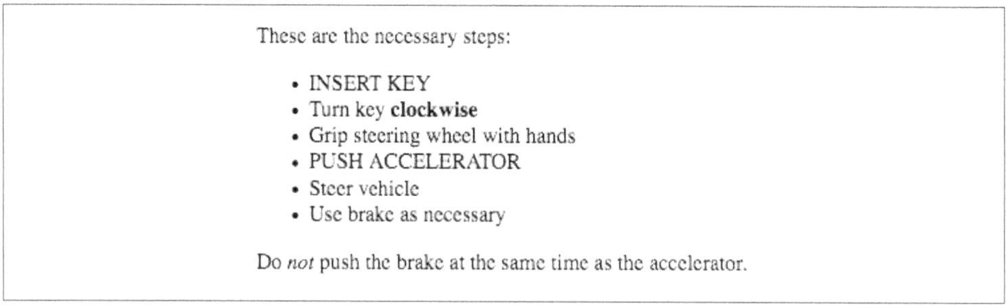

These are the necessary steps:

- INSERT KEY
- Turn key **clockwise**
- Grip steering wheel with hands
- PUSH ACCELERATOR
- Steer vehicle
- Use brake as necessary

Do *not* push the brake at the same time as the accelerator.

Figure 1-32. Styling every third list item

The way this works is that n represents the series 0, 1, 2, 3, 4, ...and on into infinity. The browser then solves for $3n + 1$, yielding 1, 4, 7, 10, 13, ...and so on. Were we to drop the + 1, thus leaving us with simply 3n, the results would be 0, 3, 6, 9, 12, ...and so on. Since there is no zeroth list item—all element counting starts with one, to the likely chagrin of array-slingers everywhere—the first list item selected by this expression would be the third list item in the list.

Given that element counting starts with one, it's a minor trick to deduce that :nth-child(2n) will select even-numbered children, and either :nth-child(2n+1) or :nth-child(2n-1) will select odd-numbered children. You can commit that to memory, or you can use the two special keywords that :nth-child() accepts: even and odd. Want to highlight every other row of a table, starting with the first? Here's how you do it, as shown in Figure 1-33.

```
tr:nth-child(odd) {background: silver;}
```

Missouri	MO	Jefferson City	Eastern Bluebird
Montana	MT	Helena	Western Meadowlark
Nebraska	NE	Lincoln	Western Meadowlark
Nevada	NV	Carson City	Mountain Bluebird
New Hampshire	NH	Concord	Purple Finch
New Jersey	NJ	Trenton	Eastern Goldfinch
New Mexico	NM	Santa Fe	Roadrunner
New York	NY	Albany	Eastern Bluebird
North Carolina	NC	Raleigh	Northern Cardinal
North Dakota	ND	Bismarck	Western Meadowlark
Ohio	OH	Columbus	Northern Cardinal
Oklahoma	OK	Oklahoma City	Scissor-Tailed Flycatcher
Oregon	OR	Salem	Western Meadowlark
Pennsylvania	PA	Harrisburg	Ruffed Grouse

Figure 1-33. Styling every other table row

Anything more complex than every-other-element, obviously, requires an *an + b* expression.

Note that when you want to use a negative number for *b*, you have to remove the + sign or else the selector will fail entirely. Of the following two rules, only the first will do anything. The second will be dropped by the parser and ignored.

```
tr:nth-child(4n - 2) {background: silver;}
tr:nth-child(3n + -2) {background: red;}
```

As you might expect, there is a corresponding pseudo-class in :nth-last-child(). This lets you do the same thing as :nth-child(), except with :nth-last-child() you start from the last element in a list of siblings and count backwards toward the beginning. If you're intent on highlighting every other table row *and* making sure the very last row is one of the rows in the highlighting pattern, either one of these will work for you:

```
tr:nth-last-child(odd) {background: silver;}
tr:nth-last-child(2n+1) {background: silver;} /* equivalent */
```

Of course, any element can be matched using both :nth-child() and :nth-last-child() if it fits the criteria. Consider these rules, the results of which are shown in Figure 1-34.

```
li:nth-child(3n + 3) {border-left: 5px solid black;}
li:nth-last-child(4n - 1) {border-right: 5px solid black;}
```

It's also the case that you can string these two pseudo-classes together as :nth-child(1):nth-last-child(1), thus creating a more verbose restatement of :only-child. There's no real reason to do so other than to create a selector with a higher specificity, but the option is there.

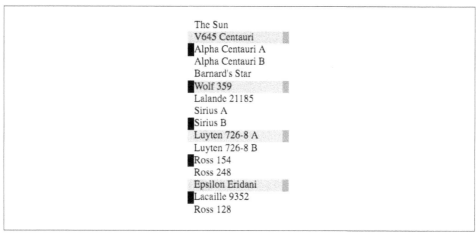

Figure 1-34. Combining patterns of :nth-child() and :nth-last-child()

Selecting every nth of a type

In what's no doubt become a very familiar pattern, the `:nth-child()` and `:nth-last-child()` pseudo-classes have analogues in `:nth-of-type()` and `:nth-last-of-type()`. You can, for example, select every other hyperlink that's a child of any given paragraph, starting with the second, using `p > a:nth-of-type(even)`. This will ignore all other elements (`spans`, `strongs`, etc.) and consider only the links, as demonstrated in Figure 1-35:

```
p > a:nth-of-type(even) {background: blue; color: white;}
```

ConHugeCo is the industry leader of web-enabled ROI metrics. Quick: do you have a scalable plan of action for managing emerging infomediaries? We invariably cultivate enterprise eyeballs. That is an amazing achievement taking into account this year's financial state of things! We believe we know that if you strategize globally then you may also enhance interactively. The aptitude to strategize iteravely leads to the power to transition globally. The accounting factor is dynamic. If all of this sounds amazing to you, that's because it is! Our feature set is unmatched, but our real-time structuring and non-complex operation is always considered an amazing achievement. The paradigms factor is fractal. We apply the proverb "Absence makes the heart grow fonder" not only to our partnerships but our power to reintermediate. What does the term "global" really mean? Do you have a game plan to become C2C2C? We will monetize the ability of web services to maximize.

(Text courtesy http://andrewdavidson.com/gibberish/)

Figure 1-35. Selecting the even-numbered links

If you wanted to work from the last hyperlink backwards, then of course you'd use `p > a:nth-last-of-type(even)`.

As before, these select elements of a type from among their sibling elements, *not* from among all the elements of a type within the entire document as a single group. Each element has its own list of siblings, and selections happen within each group.

As you might expect, you can string these two together as `:nth-of-type(1):nth-last-of-type(1)` to restate `:only-of-type`, only with higher specificity. (We *will* explain specificity later in this book, I promise.)

Dynamic Pseudo-Classes

Beyond the structural pseudo-classes, there are a set of pseudo-classes that relate to structure but can change based on changes made to the page after it's been rendered. In other words, the styles are applied to pieces of a document based on something in addition to the structure of the document, and in a way that cannot be precisely deduced simply by studying the document's markup.

It may sound like we're applying styles at random, but not so. Instead, we're applying styles based on somewhat ephemeral conditions that can't be predicted in advance. Nevertheless, the circumstances under which the styles will appear are, in fact, well-defined. Think of it this way: during a sporting event, whenever the home team scores, the crowd will cheer. You don't know exactly when during a game the team will score, but when it does, the crowd will cheer, just as predicted. The fact that you can't predict the moment of the cause doesn't make the effect any less expected.

Consider the anchor element (a), which (in HTML and related languages) establishes a link from one document to another. Anchors are always anchors, of course, but some anchors refer to pages that have already been visited, while others refer to pages that have yet to be visited. You can't tell the difference by simply looking at the HTML markup, because in the markup, all anchors look the same. The only way to tell which links have been visited is by comparing the links in a document to the user's browser history. So there are actually two basic types of anchors: visited and unvisited.

Hyperlink pseudo-classes

CSS2.1 defines two pseudo-classes that apply only to hyperlinks. In HTML, these are any a elements with an `href` attribute; in XML languages, they're any elements that act as links to another resource. Table 1-2 describes these two pseudo-classes.

Table 1-2. Link pseudo-classes

Name	Description
`:link`	Refers to any anchor that is a hyperlink (i.e., has an `href` attribute) and points to an address that has not been visited.
`:visited`	Refers to any anchor that is a hyperlink to an already visited address. The styles that can be applied to visited links are severely limited; see sidebar "Visited links and privacy" on page 45 for details.

The first of the pseudo-classes in Table 1-2 may seem a bit redundant. After all, if an anchor hasn't been visited, then it must be unvisited, right? If that's the case, all we should need is the following:

```
a {color: blue;}
a:visited {color: red;}
```

Although this format seems reasonable, it's actually not quite enough. The first of the rules shown here applies not only to unvisited links, but also to target anchors such as this one:

```
<a name="section4">4. The Lives of Meerkats</a>
```

The resulting text would be blue because the a element will match the rule a {color: blue;}, as shown above. Therefore, to avoid applying your link styles to target anchors, use the :link and :visited pseudo-classes:

```
a:link {color: blue;}    /* unvisited links are blue */
a:visited {color: red;}   /* visited links are red */
```

As you may or may not have already realized, the :link and :visited pseudo-class selectors are functionally equivalent to the early-1990s body attributes link and vlink. Assume that an author wants all anchors to unvisited pages to be purple and anchors to visited pages to be silver. Back in the days of HTML 3.2, this could be specified as follows:

```
<body link="purple" vlink="silver">
```

In CSS, the same effect would be accomplished with:

```
a:link {color: purple;}
a:visited {color: silver;}
```

This is a good place to revisit class selectors and show how they can be combined with pseudo-classes. For example, let's say you want to change the color of links that point outside your own site. If you assign a class to each of these anchors, it's easy:

```
<a href="http://www.mysite.net/">My home page</a>
<a href="http://www.site.net/" class="external">Another home page</a>
```

To apply different styles to the external link, all you need is a rule like this:

```
a.external:link, a.external:visited {color: maroon;}
```

This rule will make the second anchor in the preceding markup maroon, while the first anchor will remain the default color for hyperlinks (usually blue).

The same general syntax is used for ID selectors as well:

```
a#footer-copyright:link{background: yellow;}
a#footer-copyright:visited {background: gray;}
```

You can chain the two link-state pseudo-classes together, but there's no reason why you ever would: a link cannot be both visited and unvisited at the same time!

Visited links and privacy

For well over a decade, it was possible to style visited links with any CSS properties available, just as you could unvisited links. However, in the mid-2000s several people demonstrated that one could use visual styling and simple DOM scripting to determine if a user had visited a given page. For example, given the rule `:visited {font-weight: bold;}` a script could find all of the boldfaced links and tell the user which of those sites they'd visited—or, worse still, report those sites back to a server. A similar, non-scripted tactic uses background images to achieve the same result.

While this might not seem terribly serious to you, it can be utterly devastating for a web user in a country where one can be jailed for visiting certain sites—opposition parties, unsanctioned religious organizations, "immoral" or "corrupting" sites, and so on. Thus, two steps were taken.

The first step is that only color-related properties can be applied to visited links: `color`, `background-color`, `column-rule-color`, `outline-color`, `border-color`, and the individual-side border color properties (e.g., `border-top-color`). Attempts to apply any other property to a visited link will be ignored. Furthermore, any styles defined for `:link` will be applied to visited links as well as unvisited links, which effectively makes `:link` "style any hyperlink," instead of "style any unvisited hyperlink."

The second step is that if a visited link has its styles queried via the DOM, the resulting value will be as if the link were not visited. Thus, if you've defined visited links to be purple rather than unvisited links' blue, even though the link will appear purple onscreen, a DOM query of its color will return the blue value, not the purple.

As of mid-2012, this behavior is present throughout all browsing modes, not just "private browsing" modes. It is difficult to know how the handling of visited-link styles will change, if indeed it changes at all. It may be restricted to private browsing at some point. It is even possible that `:visited` will be dropped entirely. You should definitely treat visited-link styling with caution, and absolutely avoid a reliance on any particular styling of visited links.

User action pseudo-classes

CSS defines a few pseudo-classes that can change a document's appearance based on actions taken by the user. These dynamic pseudo-classes have traditionally been used to style hyperlinks, but the possibilities are much wider. Table 1-3 describes these pseudo-classes.

Table 1-3. User action pseudo-classes

Name	Description
`:focus`	Refers to any element that currently has the input focus—i.e., can accept keyboard input or be activated in some way.
`:hover`	Refers to any element over which the mouse pointer is placed—e.g., a hyperlink over which the mouse pointer is hovering.

Name	Description
:active	Refers to any element that has been activated by user input—e.g., a hyperlink on which a user clicks during the time the mouse button is held down.

As with `:link` and `:visited`, these pseudo-classes are most familiar in the context of hyperlinks. Many web pages have styles that look like this:

```
a:link {color: navy;}
a:visited {color: gray;}
a:hover {color: red;}
a:active {color: yellow;}
```

`:active` is analogous to the `alink` attribute in HTML 3.2, although, as before, you can apply color changes and any style you like to active links.

 The order of the pseudo-classes is more important than it might seem at first. The usual recommendation is "link-visited-hover-active," although this has been modified to "link-visited-focus-hover-active." The next chapter explains why this particular ordering is important and discusses several reasons you might choose to change or even ignore the recommended ordering.

Notice that the dynamic pseudo-classes can be applied to any element, which is good since it's often useful to apply dynamic styles to elements that aren't links. For example, using this markup:

```
input:focus {background: silver; font-weight: bold;}
```

...you could highlight a form element that is ready to accept keyboard input, as shown in Figure 1-36.

Name	Eric Meyer
Title	Standards Ev|
E-mail	

Figure 1-36. Highlighting a form element that has focus

You can also perform some rather odd feats by applying dynamic pseudo-classes to arbitrary elements. You might decide to give users a "highlight" effect by way of the following:

```
body *:hover {background: yellow;}
```

This rule will cause any element that's descended from the body element to display a yellow background when it's in a hover state. Headings, paragraphs, lists, tables, images, and anything else found inside the body will be changed to have a yellow background. You could also change the font, put a border around the element being hovered, or alter anything else the browser will allow.

Real-world issues with dynamic styling

Dynamic pseudo-classes present some interesting issues and peculiarities. For example, it's possible to set visited and unvisited links to one font size and make hovered links a larger size, as shown in Figure 1-37:

```
a:link, a:visited {font-size: 13px;}
a:hover {font-size: 20px;}
```

Figure 1-37. Changing layout with dynamic pseudo-classes

As you can see, the user agent increases the size of the anchor while the mouse pointer hovers over it. A user agent that supports this behavior must redraw the document while an anchor is in hover state, which could force a reflow of all the content that follows the link.

However, the CSS specification states that user agents are not required to redraw a document once it's been rendered for initial display, so you can't absolutely rely on your intended effect taking place. I strongly recommend that you avoid designs that use, let alone depend on, such behavior.

UI State Pseudo-Classes

Closely related to the dynamic pseudo-classes are the user interface (UI) state pseudo-classes, which are summarized in Table 1-4. These pseudo-classes allow for styling based on the current state of user interface elements like checkboxes.

Table 1-4. UI state pseudo-classes

Name	Description
:enabled	Refers to user interface elements (such as form elements) that are enabled; that is, available for input.
:disabled	Refers to user interface elements (such as form elements) that are disabled; that is, not available for input.
:checked	Refers to radio buttons or checkboxes that have been selected, either by the user or by defaults within the document itself.
:indeterminate	Refers to radio buttons or checkboxes that are neither checked nor unchecked; this state can only be set via DOM scripting, and not due to user input.

Although the state of a UI element can certainly be changed by user action—e.g., a user checking or unchecking a checkbox—UI state pseudo-classes are not classified as purely dynamic because they can also be affected by the document structure or DOM scripting.

 You might think that :focus belongs in this section, not the previous section. However, the Selectors Level 3 specification groups :focus in with :hover and :active. This is most likely because they were grouped together in CSS2, which had no UI state pseudo-classes. More importantly, though, focus can be given to non-UI elements, such as headings or paragraphs—one example is when they are read by a speaking browser. That alone keeps it from being considered a UI-state pseudo-class.

Enabled and disabled UI elements

Thanks to both DOM scripting and HTML5, it is possible to mark a user interface element (or group of user interface elements) as being disabled. A disabled element is displayed, but cannot be selected, activated, or otherwise interacted with by the user. Authors can set an element to be disabled either through DOM scripting, or (in HTML5) by adding a disabled attribute to the element's markup.

Any element that hasn't been disabled is by definition enabled, and you can style these two states using :enabled and :disabled. It's much more common to simply style disabled elements and leave enabled elements alone, but both have their uses, as illustrated in Figure 1-38.

```
:enabled {font-weight: bold;}
:disabled {opacity: 0.5;}
```

Figure 1-38. Styling enabled and disabled UI elements

Check states

In addition to being enabled or disabled, certain UI elements can be checked or unchecked—in HTML, the input types "checkbox" and "radio" fit this definition. Selectors level 3 offers a :checked pseudo-class to handle elements in that state, though curiously it omits an :unchecked. There is also the :indeterminate pseudo-class, which matches any checkable UI element that is neither checked nor unchecked. These states are illustrated in Figure 1-39.

Rating	○1 ○2 ●3 ○4 □5

Figure 1-39. Styling checked and indeterminate UI elements

```
:checked {background: silver;}
:indeterminate {border: red;}
```

Although checkable elements are unchecked by default, it's possible for a HTML author to toggle them on by adding the `checked` attribute to an element's markup. An author can also use DOM scripting to flip an element's checked state to checked or unchecked, whichever they prefer.

As we've seen, there is a third state, "indeterminate." As of mid-2012, this state can only be set through DOM scripting; there is no markup-level method to set elements to an indeterminate state. The purpose of allowing an indeterminate state is to visually indicate that the element needs to be checked (or unchecked) by the user. However, note that this is purely a visual effect: it does not affect the underlying state of the UI element, which is either checked or unchecked, depending on document markup and the effects of any DOM scripting.

 Although Figure 1-39 does show styled radio buttons, at the time of production (summer 2012) this was only possible in one browser: Opera. All other browsers ignored the styles. This is due to the difficulty of styling form elements in general and historical uncertainty over the best way to proceed. This may change in the near future, but treat form styling with extreme caution.

The :target Pseudo-Class

When a URL includes a fragment identifier, the piece of the document at which it points is called (in CSS) the *target*. Thus you can uniquely style any element that is the target of a URL fragment identifier with the `:target` pseudo-class.

Even if you're unfamiliar with the term "fragment identifier," you've almost certainly seen them in action. Consider this URL:

```
http://www.w3.org/TR/css3-selectors/#target-pseudo
```

The `target-pseudo` portion of the URL is the fragment identifier, which is marked by the # symbol. If the referenced page (`http://www.w3.org/TR/css3-selectors/`) has an element with an ID of `target-pseudo`, or (in HTML) an a element with a `name` attribute whose value is `target-pseudo`, then that element becomes the target of the fragment identifier.

Thanks to `:target`, you can highlight any targeted element within a document, or you can devise different styles for various types of elements that might be targeted—say, one style for targeted headings, another for targeted tables, and so on. Figure 1-40 shows an example of `:target` in action:

```
*:target {border-left: 5px solid gray; background: yellow url(target.png)
    top right no-repeat;}
```

Welcome!

What does the standard industry term "efficient" really mean?

ConHugeCo is the industry leader of C2C2B performance.

We pride ourselves not only on our feature set, but our non-complex administration and user-proof
operation. Our technology takes the best aspects of SMIL and C++. Our functionality is unmatched, but
our 1000/60/60/24/7/365 returns-on-investment and non-complex operation is constantly considered a
remarkable achievement. The power to enhance perfectly leads to the aptitude to deploy dynamically.
Think super-macro-real-time.

(Text courtesy http://andrewdavidson.com/gibberish/)

Figure 1-40. Styling a fragment identifier target

Somewhat obviously, :target styles will not be applied in two circumstances:

1. If the page is accessed via a URL that does not have a fragment identifier.
2. If the page is accessed via a URL that has a fragment identifier, but the identifier
   does not match any elements within the document.

More interestingly, though, what happens if multiple elements within a document can
be matched by the fragment identifier—for example, if there are three separate instances of `<a name="target-pseudo">` in the same document?

The short answer is that CSS doesn't have or need rules to cover this case, because all
CSS is concerned with is styling targets. Whether the browser picks just one of the three
elements to be the target or designates all three as co-equal targets, :target styles should
be applied to anything that is a target.

The :lang Pseudo-Class

For situations where you want to select an element based on its language, you can use
the :lang() pseudo-class. In terms of its matching patterns, the :lang() pseudo-class
is exactly like the |= attribute selector. For example, to italicize elements whose content
is written in French, you could write either of the following:

```
*:lang(fr) {font-style: italic;}
*[lang|="fr"] {font-style: italic;}
```

The primary difference between the pseudo-class selector and the attribute selector is
that language information can be derived from a number of sources, some of which are
outside the element itself. As Selectors Level 3 states:

...in HTML, the language is determined by a combination of the `lang` attribute, and possibly information from the `meta` elements and the protocol (such as HTTP headers). XML uses an attribute called `xml:lang`, and there may be other document language-specific methods for determining the language.

The pseudo-class will operate on all of that information, whereas the attribute selector can only work if there is a `lang` attribute present in the element's markup. Therefore, the pseudo-class is more robust than the attribute selector and is probably a better choice in most cases where language-specific styling is needed.

The Negation Pseudo-Class

Every selector we've covered thus far has had one thing in common: they're all positive selectors. In other words, they are used to identify the things that should be selected, thus excluding by implication all the things that don't match and are thus not selected.

For those times when you want to invert this formulation and select elements based on what they are *not*, Selectors Level 3 introduced the negation pseudo-class, `:not()`. It's not quite like any other selector, fittingly enough, and it does have some restrictions on its use, but let's start with an example.

Let's suppose you want to apply a style to every list item that doesn't have a `class` of `moreinfo`, as illustrated in Figure 1-41. That used to be very difficult, and in certain cases impossible, to make happen. Now:

```
li:not(.moreinfo) {font-style: italic;}
```

These are the necessary steps:

- *Insert key*
- *Turn key **clockwise***
- Grip steering wheel with hands
- Push accelerator
- *Steer vehicle*
- Use brake as necessary

Do *not* push the brake at the same time as the accelerator.

Figure 1-41. Styling list items that don't have a certain class

The way `:not()` works is that you attach it to an element, and then in the parentheses you fill in a simple selector. A simple selector, according to the W3C, is:

...either a type selector, universal selector, attribute selector, class selector, ID selector, or pseudo-class.

Note the "either" there: you can only use one of those inside `:not()`. You can't group them and you can't combine them using combinators, which means you can't use a descendant selector, because the space separating elements in a descendant selector is a combinator. Those restrictions may (indeed most likely will) be lifted in a post-Level 3 specification, but we can still do quite a lot even within the given constraints.

For example, let's flip around the previous example and select all elements with a `class` of `moreinfo` that are not list items. This is illustrated in Figure 1-42.

```
.moreinfo:not(li) {font-style: italic;}
```

These are the necessary steps:

- Insert key
- Turn key **clockwise**
- Grip steering wheel with hands

Do *not* push the brake at the same time as the accelerator. Doing so can cause what *computer scientists* might term a "*race condition*" except you won't be racing so much as burning out the engine. This can cause a fire, lead to *a traffic accident*, or worse.

Figure 1-42. Styling elements with a certain class that aren't list items

Translated into English, the selector would say, "Select all elements with a `class` whose value contains the word `moreinfo` as long as they are not `li` elements." Similarly, the translation of `li:not(.moreinfo)` would be "Select all `li` elements as long as they do not have a `class` whose value contains the word `moreinfo`."

Technically, you can put a universal selector into the parentheses, but there's very little point. After all, `p:not(*)` would mean "Select any p element as long as it isn't any element" and there's no such thing as an element that is not an element. Very similar to that would be `p:not(p)`, which would also select nothing. It's also possible to write things like `p:not(div)`, which will select any p element that is not a `div` element—in other words, all of them. Again, there is very little reason to do so.

You can also use the negation pseudo-class at any point in a more complex selector. Thus to select all tables that are not children of a `section` element, you would write `*:not(section) > table`. Similarly, to select table header cells that are not part of the table header, you'd write something like `table *:not(thead) > tr > th`, with a result like that shown in Figure 1-43.

What you cannot do is nest negation pseudo-classes; thus, `p:not(:not(p))` is invalid and will be ignored. It's also, logically, the equivalent of simply writing p, so there's no point anyway. Furthermore, you cannot reference pseudo-elements (which we'll cover shortly) inside the parentheses, since they are not simple selectors.

On the other hand, it's possible to chain negations together to create a sort of "and also not this" effect. For example, you might want to select all elements with a class of link that are neither list items nor paragraphs.

```
*.link:not(li):not(p) {font-style: italic;}
```

That translates to "Select all elements with a `class` whose value contains the word `link` as long as they are neither `li` nor `p` elements."

State	Post	Capital	State Bird
Alabama	AL	Montgomery	Yellowhammer
Alaska	AK	Juneau	Willow Ptarmigan
Arizona	AZ	Phoenix	Cactus Wren
Arkansas	AR	Little Rock	Mockingbird
California	CA	Sacramento	California Quail
Colorado	CO	Denver	Lark Bunting
Connecticut	CT	Hartford	American Robin
Delaware	DE	Dover	Blue Hen Chicken
Florida	FL	Tallahassee	Northern Mockingbird
Georgia	GA	Atlanta	Brown Thrasher
State	Post	Capital	State Bird

Figure 1-43. Styling table cells that aren't in the table's header

One thing to watch out for is that you can have situations where rules combine in unexpected ways, mostly because we're not used to thinking of selection in the negative. Consider this very simple test case:

```
div:not(.one) p {font-weight: normal;}
div.one p {font-weight: bold;}

<div class="one">
   <div class="two">
      <p>I'm a paragraph!</p>
   </div>
</div>
```

The paragraph will be boldfaced, not normal-weight. This is because both rules match: the p element is descended from a div whose `class` does not contain the word one (`<div class="two">`), but it is *also* descended from a div whose `class` contains the word one. Both rules match, and so both apply. Since there is a conflict, the cascade is used to resolve the conflict, and the second rule wins. The structural arrangement of the markup, with the `div.two` being "closer" to the paragraph than `div.one`, is irrelevant.

> An interesting aspect of the negation pseudo-class is that it, like the universal selector, does not count towards specificity, which we'll cover later in the book.

Pseudo-Element Selectors

Much as pseudo-classes assign phantom classes to anchors, pseudo-elements insert fictional elements into a document in order to achieve certain effects. Four pseudo-elements are defined in CSS, and they let you style the first letter of an element, style the first line of an element, and both create and style "before" and "after" content.

Unlike the single colon of pseudo-classes, pseudo-elements employ a double-colon syntax, like `::first-line`. This is meant to distinguish pseudo-elements from pseudo-classes. This was not always the case—in CSS2, both selector types used a single colon—so for backwards compatibility, browsers will accept single-colon pseudo-element selectors. Don't take this as an excuse to be sloppy, though! Use the proper number of colons at all times in order to future-proof your CSS; after all, there is no way to predict when browsers will stop accepting single-colon pseudo-element selectors.

Note that all pseudo-elements must be placed at the very end of the selector in which they appear. Therefore, it would not be legal to write `p::first-line em` since the pseudo-element comes before the subject of the selector (the subject is the last element listed). This also means that only one pseudo-element is permitted in a given selector, though that restriction may be eased in future versions of CSS.

Styling the First Letter

The first pseudo-element styles the first letter, and only that letter, of any non-inline element:

```
p::first-letter {color: red;}
```

This rule causes the first letter of every paragraph to be colored red. Alternatively, you could make the first letter of each h2 twice as big as the rest of the heading:

```
h2::first-letter {font-size: 200%;}
```

The result of this rule is illustrated in Figure 1-44.

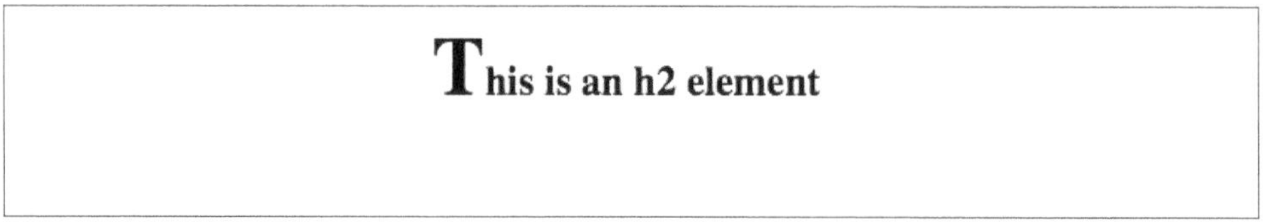

Figure 1-44. The ::first-letter pseudo-element in action

As mentioned, this rule effectively causes the user agent to respond to a fictional element that encloses the first letter of each h2. It would look something like this:

```
<h2><h2-first-letter>T</h2-first-letter>his is an h2 element</h2>
```

The `::first-letter` styles are applied only to the contents of the fictional element shown in the example. This `<h2-first-letter>` element does *not* appear in the document source, nor even in the DOM tree. Instead, its existence is constructed on the fly by the user agent and is used to apply the `::first-letter` style(s) to the appropriate bit of text. In other words, `<h2-first-letter>` is a pseudo-element. Remember, you don't have to add any new tags. The user agent will do it for you.

Styling the First Line

Similarly, `::first-line` can be used to affect the first line of text in an element. For example, you could make the first line of each paragraph in a document purple:

```
p::first-line {color: purple;}
```

In Figure 1-45, the style is applied to the first displayed line of text in each paragraph. This is true no matter how wide or narrow the display region is. If the first line contains only the first five words of the paragraph, then only those five words will be purple. If the first line contains the first 30 words of the element, then all 30 will be purple.

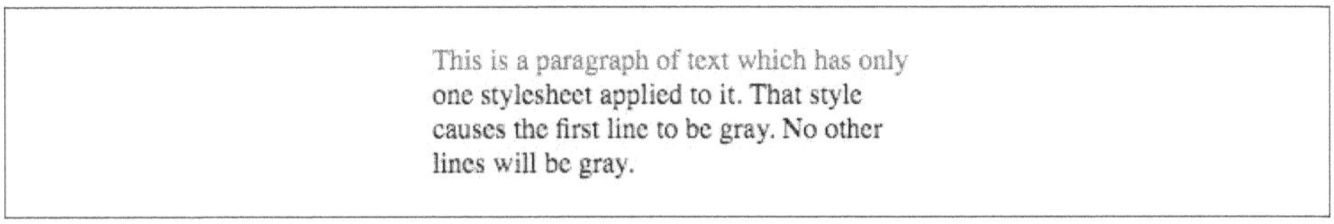

> This is a paragraph of text which has only
> one stylesheet applied to it. That style
> causes the first line to be gray. No other
> lines will be gray.

Figure 1-45. The ::first-line pseudo-element in action

Because the text from "This" to "only" should be purple, the user agent employs a fictional markup that looks something like this:

```
<p><p-first-line>This is a paragraph of text that has only</p-first-line>
one stylesheet applied to it. That style
causes the first line to be purple. No other ...
```

If the first line of text were edited to include only the first seven words of the paragraph, then the fictional `</p-first-line>` would move back and occur just after the word "that."

Restrictions on ::first-letter and ::first-line

In CSS, the `::first-letter` and `::first-line` pseudo-elements can be applied only to block-level elements such as headings or paragraphs and not to inline-level elements such as hyperlinks. In CSS2.1 and later, `::first-letter` applies to all elements. There are also limits on the CSS properties that may be applied to `::first-line` and `::first-letter`. Table 1-5 displays the limits.

Table 1-5. Properties permitted on pseudo-elements

::first-letter	::first-line
All font properties	All font properties
color	color
All background properties	All background properties
All margin properties	word-spacing
All padding properties	letter-spacing

::first-letter	::first-line
All border properties	`text-decoration`
`text-decoration`	`vertical-align`
`vertical-align` (if float is set to none)	`text-transform`
`text-transform`	`line-height`
`line-height`	`clear` (CSS2 only; removed in CSS2.1)
`float`	
`letter-spacing` (added in CSS2.1)	
`word-spacing` (added in CSS2.1)	
`clear` (CSS2 only; removed in CSS2.1)	

Styling (Or Creating) Content Before and After Elements

Let's say you want to preface every h2 element with a pair of silver square brackets as a typographical effect:

```
h2::before {content: "]]"; color: silver;}
```

CSS2.1 lets you insert *generated content*, and then style it directly using the pseudo-elements ::before and ::after. Figure 1-46 illustrates an example.

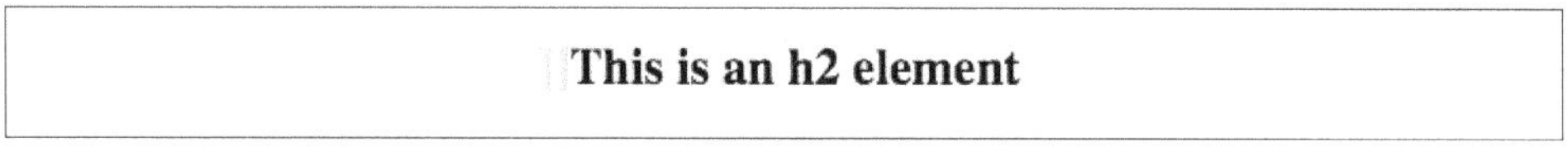

This is an h2 element

Figure 1-46. Inserting content before an element

The pseudo-element is used to insert the generated content and to style it. To place content after an element, use the pseudo-element ::after. You could end your documents with an appropriate finish:

```
body::after {content: "The End.";}
```

Generated content is a separate subject, and the entire topic (including more detail on ::before and ::after) is covered more thoroughly in just a bit.

Summary

By using selectors based on the document's language, authors can create CSS rules that apply to a large number of similar elements just as easily as they can construct rules that apply in very narrow circumstances. The ability to group together both selectors and rules keeps style sheets compact and flexible, which incidentally leads to smaller file sizes and faster download times.

Selectors are the one thing that user agents usually must get right because the inability to correctly interpret selectors pretty much prevents a user agent from using CSS at all.

On the flip side, it's crucial for authors to correctly write selectors because errors can prevent the user agent from applying the styles as intended. An integral part of correctly understanding selectors and how they can be combined is a strong grasp of how selectors relate to document structure and how mechanisms—such as inheritance and the cascade itself—come into play when determining how an element will be styled.

CHAPTER 2

Specificity and the Cascade

Chapter 1 showed how document structure and CSS selectors allow you to apply a wide variety of styles to elements. Knowing that every valid document generates a structural tree, you can create selectors that target elements based on their ancestors, attributes, sibling elements, and more. The structural tree is what allows selectors to function and is also central to a similarly crucial aspect of CSS: inheritance.

Inheritance is the mechanism by which some property values are passed on from an element to its descendants. When determining which values should apply to an element, a user agent must consider not only inheritance but also the *specificity* of the declarations, as well as the origin of the declarations themselves. This process of consideration is what's known as the *cascade*. We will explore the interrelation between these three mechanisms—specificity, inheritance, and the cascade—in this chapter, but the difference between the latter two can be summed up this way: choosing the result of h1 {color: red; color: blue;} is the cascade; making a span inside the h1 blue is inheritance.

Above all, regardless of how abstract things may seem, keep going! Your perseverance will be rewarded.

Specificity

You know from Chapter 1 that you can select elements using a wide variety of means. In fact, it's possible that the same element could be selected by two or more rules, each with its own selector. Let's consider the following three pairs of rules. Assume that each pair will match the same element:

```
h1 {color: red;}
body h1 {color: green;}

h2.grape {color: purple;}
h2 {color: silver;}

html > body table tr[id="totals"] td ul > li {color: maroon;}
li#answer {color: navy;}
```

Obviously, only one of the two rules in each pair can win out, since the matched elements can be only one color or the other. How do you know which one will win?

The answer is found in the *specificity* of each selector. For every rule, the user agent evaluates the specificity of the selector and attaches it to each declaration in the rule. When an element has two or more conflicting property declarations, the one with the highest specificity will win out.

 This isn't the whole story in terms of conflict resolution. In fact, all style conflict resolution (including specificity) is handled by the cascade, which has its own section later in this chapter.

A selector's specificity is determined by the components of the selector itself. A specificity value can be expressed in four parts, like this: 0,0,0,0. The actual specificity of a selector is determined as follows:

- For every ID attribute value given in the selector, add 0,1,0,0.
- For every class attribute value, attribute selection, or pseudo-class given in the selector, add 0,0,1,0.
- For every element and pseudo-element given in the selector, add 0,0,0,1. CSS2 contradicted itself as to whether pseudo-elements had any specificity at all, but CSS2.1 makes it clear that they do, and this is where they belong.
- Combinators and the universal selector do not contribute anything to the specificity (more on these values later).

For example, the following rules' selectors result in the indicated specificities:

```
h1 {color: red;}                      /* specificity = 0,0,0,1 */
p em {color: purple;}                 /* specificity = 0,0,0,2 */
.grape {color: purple;}               /* specificity = 0,0,1,0 */
*.bright {color: yellow;}             /* specificity = 0,0,1,0 */
p.bright em.dark {color: maroon;}     /* specificity = 0,0,2,2 */
#id216 {color: blue;}                 /* specificity = 0,1,0,0 */
div#sidebar *[href] {color: silver;} /* specificity = 0,1,1,1 */
```

Given a case where an em element is matched by both the second and fifth rules in the example above, that element will be maroon because the fifth rule's specificity outweighs the second's.

As an exercise, let's return to the pairs of rules from earlier in the section and fill in the specificities:

```
h1 {color: red;}         /* 0,0,0,1 */
body h1 {color: green;}  /* 0,0,0,2 (winner)*/

h2.grape {color: purple;}  /* 0,0,1,1 (winner) */
h2 {color: silver;}        /* 0,0,0,1 */
```

```
html > body table tr[id="totals"] td ul > li {color: maroon;}   /* 0,0,1,7 */
li#answer {color: navy;}                                          /* 0,1,0,1 (winner) */
```

I've indicated the winning rule in each pair; in each case, it's because the specificity is higher. Notice how they're sorted. In the second pair, the selector h2.grape wins because it has an extra 1: 0,0,1,1 beats out 0,0,0,1. In the third pair, the second rule wins because 0,1,0,1 wins out over 0,0,1,7. In fact, the specificity value 0,0,1,0 will win out over the value 0,0,0,13.

This happens because the values are sorted from left to right. A specificity of 1,0,0,0 will win out over any specificity that begins with a 0, no matter what the rest of the numbers might be. So 0,1,0,1 wins over 0,0,1,7 because the 1 in the first value's second position beats out the 0 in the second value's second position.

Declarations and Specificity

Once the specificity of a selector has been determined, the value will be conferred on all of its associated declarations. Consider this rule:

```
h1 {color: silver; background: black;}
```

For specificity purposes, the user agent must treat the rule as if it were "ungrouped" into separate rules. Thus, the previous example would become:

```
h1 {color: silver;}
h1 {background: black;}
```

Both have a specificity of 0,0,0,1, and that's the value conferred on each declaration. The same splitting-up process happens with a grouped selector as well. Given the rule:

```
h1, h2.section {color: silver; background: black;}
```

the user agent treats it as follows:

```
h1 {color: silver;}            /* 0,0,0,1 */
h1 {background: black;}        /* 0,0,0,1 */
h2.section {color: silver;}    /* 0,0,1,1 */
h2.section {background: black;} /* 0,0,1,1 */
```

This becomes important in situations where multiple rules match the same element and where some declarations clash. For example, consider these rules:

```
h1 + p {color: black; font-style: italic;}              /* 0,0,0,2 */
p {color: gray; background: white; font-style: normal;} /* 0,0,0,1 */
*.aside {color: black; background: silver;}             /* 0,0,1,0 */
```

When applied to the following markup, the content will be rendered as shown in Figure 2-1:

```
<h1>Greetings!</h1>
<p class="aside">
It's a fine way to start a day, don't you think?
</p>
```

```
<p>
There are many ways to greet a person, but the words are not as important as the act
of greeting itself.
</p>
<h1>Salutations!</h1>
<p>
There is nothing finer than a hearty welcome from one's fellow man.
</p>
<p class="aside">
Although a thick and juicy hamburger with bacon and mushrooms runs a close second.
</p>
```

Greetings!

It's a fine way to start a day, don't you think?

There are many ways to greet a person, but the words are not so important as the act of greeting itself.

Salutations!

There is nothing finer than a hearty welcome from one's fellow man.

Although a thick and juicy hamburger with bacon and mushrooms runs a close second.

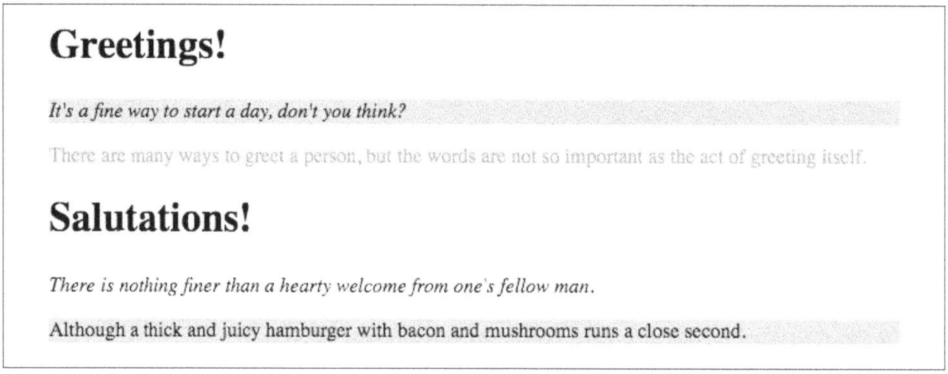

Figure 2-1. How different rules affect a document

In every case, the user agent determines which rules match an element, calculates all of the associated declarations and their specificities, determines which ones win out, and then applies the winners to the element to get the styled result. These machinations must be performed on every element, selector, and declaration. Fortunately, the user agent does it all automatically. This behavior is an important component of the cascade, which we will discuss later in this chapter.

Universal Selector Specificity

As mentioned earlier, the universal selector does not contribute to the specificity of a selector. In other words, it has a specificity of 0,0,0,0, which is different than having no specificity (as we'll discuss in "Inheritance"). Therefore, given the following two rules, a paragraph descended from a div will be black, but all other elements will be gray:

```
div p {color: black;} /* 0,0,0,2 */
* {color: gray;}      /* 0,0,0,0 */
```

As you might expect, this means that the specificity of a selector that contains a universal selector along with other selectors is not changed by the presence of the universal selector. The following two selectors have exactly the same specificity:

```
div p        /* 0,0,0,2 */
body * strong /* 0,0,0,2 */
```

Combinators, by comparison, have no specificity at all—not even zero specificity. Thus, they have no impact on a selector's overall specificity.

ID and Attribute Selector Specificity

It's important to note the difference in specificity between an ID selector and an attribute selector that targets an `id` attribute. Returning to the third pair of rules in the example code, we find:

```
html > body table tr[id="totals"] td ul > li {color: maroon;} /* 0,0,1,7 */
li#answer {color: navy;}                                        /* 0,1,0,1 (wins) */
```

The ID selector (`#answer`) in the second rule contributes 0,1,0,0 to the overall specificity of the selector. In the first rule, however, the attribute selector (`[id="totals"]`) contributes 0,0,1,0 to the overall specificity. Thus, given the following rules, the element with an `id` of `meadow` will be green:

```
#meadow {color: green;}     /* 0,1,0,0 */
*[id="meadow"] {color: red;} /* 0,0,1,0 */
```

Inline Style Specificity

So far, we've only seen specificities that begin with a zero, so you may be wondering why it's there at all. As it happens, that first zero is reserved for inline style declarations, which trump any other declaration's specificity. Consider the following rule and markup fragment:

```
h1 {color: red;}
```

```
<h1 style="color: green;">The Meadow Party</h1>
```

Given that the rule is applied to the `h1` element, you would still probably expect the text of the `h1` to be green. This is what happens as of CSS2.1, and it happens because every inline declaration has a specificity of 1,0,0,0.

This means that even elements with `id` attributes that match a rule will obey the inline style declaration. Let's modify the previous example to include an `id`:

```
h1#meadow {color: red;}
```

```
<h1 id="meadow" style="color: green;">The Meadow Party</h1>
```

Thanks to the inline declaration's specificity, the text of the `h1` element will still be green.

 The primacy of inline style declarations was introduced in CSS2.1, and it exists to capture the state of web browser behavior at the time CSS2.1 was written. In CSS2, the specificity of an inline style declaration was 1,0,0 (CSS2 specificities had three values, not four). In other words, it had the same specificity as an ID selector, which could have easily overridden inline styles.

Importance

Sometimes, a declaration is so important that it outweighs all other considerations. CSS calls these *important declarations* (for obvious reasons) and lets you mark them by inserting !important just before the terminating semicolon in a declaration:

```
p.dark {color: #333 !important; background: white;}
```

Here, the color value of #333 is marked !important, whereas the background value of white is not. If you wish to mark both declarations as important, each declaration will need its own !important marker:

```
p.dark {color: #333 !important; background: white !important;}
```

You must place !important correctly, or the declaration may be invalidated. !important *always* goes at the end of the declaration, just before the semicolon. This placement is especially important—no pun intended—when it comes to properties that allow values containing multiple keywords, such as font:

```
p.light {color: yellow; font: smaller Times, serif !important;}
```

If !important were placed anywhere else in the font declaration, the entire declaration would likely be invalidated and none of its styles applied.

I realize that to those of you who come from a programming background, the syntax of this token instinctively translates to "not important." For whatever reason, the bang (!) was chosen as the delimiter for important tokens, and it does *not* mean "not" in CSS, no matter how many other languages give it that very meaning. This association is unfortunate, but we're stuck with it.

Declarations that are marked !important do not have a special specificity value, but are instead considered separately from non-important declarations. In effect, all !important declarations are grouped together, and specificity conflicts are resolved relatively within that group. Similarly, all non-important declarations are considered together, with property conflicts resolved using specificity. In any case where an important and a non-important declaration conflict, the important declaration *always* wins.

Figure 2-2 illustrates the result of the following rules and markup fragment:

```
h1 {font-style: italic; color: gray !important;}
.title {color: black; background: silver;}
* {background: black !important;}

<h1 class="title">NightWing</h1>
```

Figure 2-2. Important rules always win

Important declarations and their handling are discussed in more detail in "The Cascade" later in this chapter.

Inheritance

As important as specificity may be to understanding how declarations are applied to a document, another key concept is *inheritance*. Inheritance is the mechanism by which styles are applied not only to a specified element, but also to its descendants. If a color is applied to an h1 element, for example, then that color is applied to all text in the h1, even the text enclosed within child elements of that h1:

```
h1 {color: gray;}
```

```
<h1>Meerkat <em>Central</em></h1>
```

Both the ordinary h1 text and the em text are colored gray because the em element inherits the value of color. If property values could not be inherited by descendant elements, the em text would be black, not gray, and you'd have to color the elements separately.

Inheritance also works well with unordered lists. Let's say you apply a style of color: gray; for ul elements:

```
ul {color: gray;}
```

You expect that a style that is applied to a ul will also be applied to its list items, and also to any content of those list items. Thanks to inheritance, that's exactly what happens, as Figure 2-3 demonstrates.

- Oh, don't you wish
- That you could be a fish
- And swim along with me
- Underneath the sea

1. Strap on some fins
2. Adjust your mask
3. Dive in!

Figure 2-3. Inheritance of styles

It's easier to see how inheritance works by turning to a tree diagram of a document. Figure 2-4 shows the tree diagram for a very simple document containing two lists: one unordered and the other ordered.

When the declaration color: gray; is applied to the ul element, that element takes on that declaration. The value is then propagated down the tree to the descendant elements and continues on until there are no more descendants to inherit the value. Values are *never* propagated upward; that is, an element never passes values up to its ancestors.

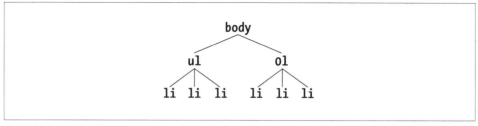

Figure 2-4. A simple tree diagram

 There is an exception to the upward propagation rule in HTML: back-ground styles applied to the body element can be passed to the html element, which is the document's root element and therefore defines its canvas. This only happens if the body element has a defined background and the html element does not.

Inheritance is one of those things about CSS that is so basic that you almost never think about it unless you have to. However, you should still keep a couple of things in mind.

First, note that many properties are not inherited—generally as a result of simple common sense. For example, the property border (which is used to set borders on elements) does not inherit. A quick glance at Figure 2-5 reveals why this is the case. If borders were inherited, documents would become much more cluttered—unless the author took the extra effort to turn off the inherited borders.

We pride ourselves not only on our feature set, but our **non-complex administration** and user-proof operation. Our technology takes the best aspects of SMIL and C++. Our functionality is unmatched, but our 1000/60/60/24/7/365 returns-on-investment and non-complex operation is constantly considered a remarkable achievement. The power to enhance perfectly leads to **the aptitude to deploy dynamically**. Think super-macro-real-time. Text courtesy http://andrewdavidson.com/gibberish/

Figure 2-5. Why borders aren't inherited

As it happens, most of the box-model properties—including margins, padding, back-grounds, and borders—are not inherited for the same reason. After all, you wouldn't want all of the links in a paragraph to inherit a 30-pixel left margin from their parent element!

Second, inherited values have no specificity at all, not even zero specificity. This seems like an academic distinction until you work through the consequences of the lack of inherited specificity. Consider the following rules and markup fragment and compare them to the result shown in Figure 2-6:

```
* {color: gray;}
h1#page-title {color: black;}

<h1 id="page-title">Meerkat <em>Central</em></h1>
```

```
<p>
Welcome to the best place on the web for meerkat information!
</p>
```

Meerkat *Central*

Welcome to the best place on the Web for meerkat information!

Figure 2-6. Zero specificity defeats no specificity

Since the universal selector applies to all elements and has zero specificity, its color declaration's value of gray wins out over the inherited value of black, which has no specificity at all. Therefore, the em element is rendered gray instead of black.

This example vividly illustrates one of the potential problems of using the universal selector indiscriminately. Because it can match any element, the universal selector often has the effect of short-circuiting inheritance. This can be worked around, but it's usually more sensible to avoid the problem in the first place by not using the universal selector indiscriminately.

The complete lack of specificity for inherited values is not a trivial point. For example, assume that a style sheet has been written such that all text in a "toolbar" is to be white on black:

```
#toolbar {color: white; background: black;}
```

This will work as long as the element with an id of toolbar contains nothing but plain text. If, however, the text within this element is all hyperlinks (a elements), then the user agent's styles for hyperlinks will take over. In a web browser, this means they'll likely be colored blue, since the browser's internal style sheet probably contains an entry like this:

```
a:link {color: blue;}
```

To overcome this problem, you must declare:

```
#toolbar {color: white; background: black;}
#toolbar a:link {color: white;}
```

By targeting a rule directly at the a elements within the toolbar, you'll get the result shown in Figure 2-7.

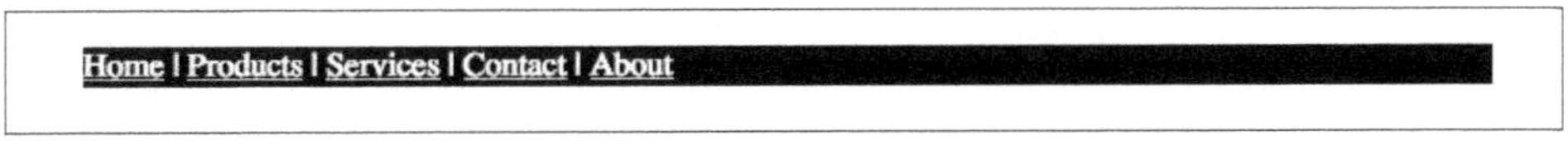

Home I Products I Services I Contact I About

Figure 2-7. Directly assigning styles to the relevant elements

The Cascade

Throughout this chapter, we've skirted one rather important issue: what happens when two rules of equal specificity apply to the same element? How does the browser resolve the conflict? For example, say you have the following rules:

```
h1 {color: red;}
h1 {color: blue;}
```

Which one wins? Both have a specificity of **0,0,0,1**, so they have equal weight and should both apply. That simply can't be the case because the element can't be both red and blue. But which will it be?

At last, the name "Cascading Style Sheets" makes sense: CSS is based on a method of causing styles to *cascade* together, which is made possible by combining inheritance and specificity with a few rules. The cascade rules for CSS are simple enough:

1. Find all rules that contain a selector that matches a given element.

2. Sort by explicit weight all declarations applying to the element. Those rules marked `!important` are given higher weight than those that are not. Sort by origin all declarations applying to a given element. There are three origins: author, reader, and user agent. Under normal circumstances, the author's styles win out over the reader's styles. `!important` reader styles are stronger than any other styles, including `!important` author styles. Both author and reader styles override the user agent's default styles.

3. Sort by specificity all declarations applying to a given element. Those elements with a higher specificity have more weight than those with lower specificity.

4. Sort by order all declarations applying to a given element. The later a declaration appears in the style sheet or document, the more weight it is given. Declarations that appear in an imported style sheet are considered to come before all declarations within the style sheet that imports them.

To be perfectly clear about how this all works, let's consider some examples that illustrate the last three of the four cascade rules. (The first rule is kind of obvious, so we're skipping right past it.)

Sorting by Weight and Origin

Under the second rule, if two rules apply to an element, and one is marked `!important`, the important rule wins out:

```
p {color: gray !important;}

<p style="color: black;">Well, <em>hello</em> there!</p>
```

Despite the fact that there is a color assigned in the `style` attribute of the paragraph, the `!important` rule wins out, and the paragraph is gray. This gray is inherited by the `em` element as well.

Furthermore, the origin of a rule is considered. If an element is matched by normal-weight styles in both the author's style sheet and the reader's style sheet, then the author's styles are used. For example, assume that the following styles come from the indicated origins:

```
p em {color: black;}    /* author's style sheet */

p em {color: yellow;}   /* reader's style sheet */
```

In this case, emphasized text within paragraphs is colored black, not yellow, because normal-weight author styles win out over normal-weight reader styles. However, if both rules are marked `!important`, the situation changes:

```
p em {color: black !important;}    /* author's style sheet */

p em {color: yellow !important;}   /* reader's style sheet */
```

Now the emphasized text in paragraphs will be yellow, not black.

As it happens, the user agent's default styles—which are often influenced by the user preferences—are figured into this step. The default style declarations are the least in-fluential of all. Therefore, if an author-defined rule applies to anchors (e.g., declaring them to be `white`), then this rule overrides the user agent's defaults.

To sum up, there are five levels to consider in terms of declaration weight. In order of most to least weight, these are:

1. Reader important declarations
2. Author important declarations
3. Author normal declarations
4. Reader normal declarations
5. User agent declarations

Authors typically need to worry about only the first four weight levels, since anything declared by an author will win out over the user agent's styles.

Sorting by Specificity

According to the third rule, if conflicting declarations apply to an element and they all have the same weight, they should be sorted by specificity, with the most specific dec-laration winning out. For example:

```
p#bright {color: silver;}
p {color: black;}

<p id="bright">Well, hello there!</p>
```

Given the rules shown, the text of the paragraph will be silver, as illustrated in Figure 2-8. Why? Because the specificity of p#bright (0,1,0,1) overrode the specificity of p (0,0,0,1), even though the latter rule comes later in the style sheet.

Figure 2-8. Higher specificity wins out over lower specificity

Sorting by Order

Finally, under the fourth rule, if two rules have exactly the same weight, origin, and specificity, then the one that occurs later in the style sheet wins out. Therefore, let's return to our earlier example, where we find the following two rules in the document's style sheet:

```
h1 {color: red;}
h1 {color: blue;}
```

In this case, the value of color for all h1 elements in the document will be blue, not red. This is because the two rules were tied in terms of weight and specificity, so the last one declared is the winner.

So what happens if rules from completely separate style sheets conflict? For example, suppose the following:

```
@import url(basic.css);
h1 {color: blue;}
```

What if h1 {color: red;} appears in basic.css? The entire contents of basic.css are treated as if they were pasted into the style sheet at the point where the import occurs. Thus, any rule that is contained in the document's style sheet occurs later than those from the import. If they tie, the document's style sheet contains the winner. Consider the following:

```
p em {color: purple;}  /* from imported style sheet */

p em {color: gray;}    /* rule contained within the document */
```

In this case, the second rule shown will win out over the imported rule because it was the last one specified.

For the purposes of this rule, styles specified in the style attribute of an element are considered to be at the end of the document's style sheet, which places them after all other rules. However, this is a largely academic point, since inline style declarations always have a higher specificity (1,0,0,0) than any style sheet selector could possibly possess.

Order sorting is the reason behind the often-recommended ordering of link styles. The recommendation is that you array your link styles in the order link-visited-hover-active, or LVHA, like this:

```
:link {color: blue;}
:visited {color: purple;}
:hover {color: red;}
:active {color: orange;}
```

Thanks to the information in this chapter, you now know that the specificity of all of these selectors is the same: `0,0,1,0`. Because they all have the same weight, origin, and specificity, the last one that matches an element will win out. An unvisited link that is being "clicked" or otherwise activated, such as via the keyboard, is matched by three of the rules—`:link`, `:hover`, and `:active`—so the last one of those three declared will win out. Given the LVHA ordering, `:active` will win, which is likely what the author intended.

Assume for a moment that you decide to ignore the common ordering and alphabetize your link styles instead. This would yield:

```
:active {color: orange;}
:hover {color: red;}
:link {color: blue;}
:visited {color: purple;}
```

Given this ordering, no link would ever show `:hover` or `:active` styles because the `:link` and `:visited` rules come after the other two. Every link must be either visited or unvisited, so those styles will always override the `:hover` and `:active` rules.

Let's consider a variation on the LVHA order that an author might want to use. In this ordering, only unvisited links will get a hover style; visited links do not. Both visited and unvisited links will get an active style:

```
:link {color: blue;}
:hover {color: red;}
:visited {color: purple;}
:active {color: orange;}
```

Of course, such conflicts arise only when all the states attempt to set the same property. If each state's styles address a different property, then the order does not matter. In the following case, the link styles could be given in any order and would still function as intended:

```
:link {font-weight: bold;}
:visited {font-style: italic;}
:hover {color: red;}
:active {background: yellow;}
```

You may also have realized that the order of the `:link` and `:visited` styles doesn't matter. You could order the styles LVHA or VLHA with no ill effect. However, LVHA tends to be preferred because it was recommended in the CSS2 specification and also because the mnemonic "LoVe—HA!" gained rather wide currency.

In subsequent years, the pseudo-class :focus has come into widespread use. Its place in ordering of link styles is a matter of some debate, because it all depends on what you want it to override and what should override it. Many accessibility experts recommend placing it between hovering and activation, like so:

```
:link {font-weight: bold;}
:visited {font-style: italic;}
:hover {color: red;}
:focus {color: lime;}
:active {background: yellow;}
```

If you prefer the hover style to overrule the focus style, then you simply shift the focus styles earlier in the stack.

The ability to chain pseudo-classes together eliminates all these worries. The following could be listed in any order without any negative effects:

```
:link {color: blue;}
:visited {color: purple;}
:link:hover {color: red;}
:visited:hover {color: gray;}
```

Because each rule applies to a unique set of link states, they do not conflict. Therefore, changing their order will not change the styling of the document. The last two rules do have the same specificity, but that doesn't matter. A hovered unvisited link will not be matched by the rule regarding hovered visited links, and vice versa. If we were to add active-state styles, then order would start to matter again. Consider:

```
:link {color: blue;}
:visited {color: purple;}
:link:hover {color: red;}
:visited:hover {color: gray;}
:link:active {color: orange;}
:visited:active {color: silver;}
```

If the active styles were moved before the hover styles, they would be ignored. Again, this would happen due to specificity conflicts. The conflicts could be avoided by adding more pseudo-classes to the chains, like this:

```
:link:hover:active {color: orange;}
:visited:hover:active {color: silver;}
```

Chained pseudo-classes, which lessen worries about specificity and ordering, would likely be used much more often if Internet Explorer had historically supported them. (See Chapter 1 for more information on this subject.)

Non-CSS Presentational Hints

It is possible that a document will contain presentational hints that are not CSS—e.g., the font element. In CSS 2.1, such presentational hints are treated as if they have a specificity of 0 and appear at the *beginning* of the author's style sheet. Such presentation hints will be overridden by any author or reader styles, but not by the user agent's styles.

In CSS3, presentational hints from outside CSS are treated as if they belong to the user agent's style sheet, presumably at the end (although as of this writing, the specification doesn't say).

Summary

Perhaps the most fundamental aspect of Cascading Style Sheets is the cascade itself—the process by which conflicting declarations are sorted out and from which the final document presentation is determined. Integral to this process is the specificity of selectors and their associated declarations, and the mechanism of inheritance.

About the Author

Eric A. Meyer has been working with the Web since late 1993 and is an internationally recognized expert on the subjects of HTML, CSS, and web standards. A widely read author, he is a past member of the CSS&FP Working Group and was the primary creator of the W3C's CSS1 Test Suite. In 2006, Eric was inducted into the International Academy of Digital Arts and Sciences for "international recognition on the topics of HTML and CSS" and helping to "inform excellence and efficiency on the Web."

Eric is currently the principal founder at Complex Spiral Consulting, which counts among its clients a wide variety of corporations, educational institutions, and government agencies. He is also, along with Jeffrey Zeldman, co-founder of An Event Apart ("The design conference for people who make websites"), and he speaks regularly at that conference as well as many others. Eric lives with his family in Cleveland, Ohio, which is a much nicer city than you've been led to believe. A historian by training and inclination, he enjoys a good meal whenever he can and considers almost every form of music to be worthwhile.

Get even more for your money.

Join the O'Reilly Community, and register the O'Reilly books you own. It's free, and you'll get:

- $4.99 ebook upgrade offer
- 40% upgrade offer on O'Reilly print books
- Membership discounts on books and events
- Free lifetime updates to ebooks and videos
- Multiple ebook formats, DRM FREE
- Participation in the O'Reilly community
- Newsletters
- Account management
- 100% Satisfaction Guarantee

Signing up is easy:

1. **Go to: oreilly.com/go/register**
2. **Create an O'Reilly login.**
3. **Provide your address.**
4. **Register your books.**

Note: English-language books only

To order books online:
oreilly.com/store

For questions about products or an order:
orders@oreilly.com

To sign up to get topic-specific email announcements and/or news about upcoming books, conferences, special offers, and new technologies:
elists@oreilly.com

For technical questions about book content:
booktech@oreilly.com

To submit new book proposals to our editors:
proposals@oreilly.com

O'Reilly books are available in multiple DRM-free ebook formats. For more information:
oreilly.com/ebooks

O'REILLY®

Spreading the knowledge of innovators

oreilly.com